# MARCO ⊕ POLO

# MAURITIUS

MALDIVES

SEYCHELLES

Chagos Isl.
(GB)

COMOROS

INDIAN

MAURITIUS

OCEAN

MADA-
GASCAR

Port Louis

www.marco-polo.com

**SYMBOLS**

| | |
|---|---|
| **INSIDER TIP** | Insider Tip |
| ★ | Highlight |
| ●●●● | Best of ... |
| ⚶ | Scenic view |
| ☺ | Responsible travel: fair trade principles and the environment respected |
| (*) | Telephone numbers that are not toll-free |

**PRICE CATEGORIES
HOTELS**

*Expensive*   over 5,200 rupees

*Moderate*   3,200 – 5,200 rupees

*Budget*   under 3,200 rupees

Prices are based on two people sharing a double room
per night with half board

**PRICE CATEGORIES
RESTAURANTS**

*Expensive*   over 1,400 rupees

*Moderate*   800 – 1,400 rupees

*Budget*   under 800 rupees

Prices are based on a three-
course à la carte menu including drinks

On the cover: Botanical Garden p. 38 | Strolling under the water in Grand Baie p. 35, 95

# CONTENTS

The East → p. 58

The South West → p. 68

The West → p. 76

Road atlas → p. 116

**DID YOU KNOW?**
Timeline → p. 12
Local specialities → p. 26
Mountain walks → p. 56
Books & Films → p. 66
Budgeting → p. 105
Currency converter → p. 106
Weather in Mauritius → p. 109

**MAPS IN THE GUIDEBOOK**
(118 A1) Page numbers and
coordinates refer to the road
atlas
(0) Site/address located off
the map.
Coordinates are also given for
places that are not marked
on the road atlas
(U A1) Refers to the map of
Port Louis in the back cover

**INSIDE BACK COVER:
PULL-OUT MAP →**

**PULL-OUT MAP** 🔖
(🔖 A–B 2–3) Refers to the
removable pull-out map
(🔖 a–b 2–3) Refers to additional inset maps on the
pull-out map

2 | 3

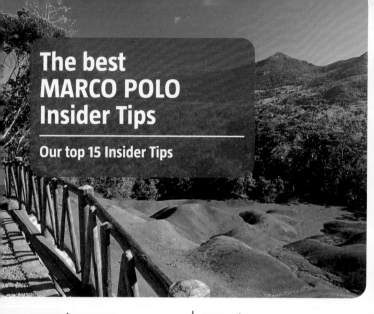

# The best MARCO POLO Insider Tips

## Our top 15 Insider Tips

**INSIDERTIP** **A freshly brewed flavour**

Direct from the plantation to your cup: after a tour, the secrets of how these aromatic, delicate leaves are cultivated will be revealed to you during a tasting session in the Bois Chéri Tea Factory → **p. 75**

**INSIDERTIP** **Shimmering earth**

The ground glows with colours that range from red to blue and purple to ochre: this patch of earth with its fascinating shades came to light in the Vallée des 23 Couleurs during construction work in 1998. It's a colourful illustration of Mauritius' volcanic past (photo left) → **p. 75**

**INSIDERTIP** **À la mode de Paris**

Whether it's colourful fabrics and unusual materials you're after, or chic jeans and other reasonably priced items, bargain hunters will find the very thing at the Quatre Borne clothes market. Woven straw bags and souvenirs are also on offer → **p. 82**

**INSIDERTIP** **A paradise for surfing freaks**

Secret tip number 1 for windsurfers and kitesurfers is the area around Morne Brabant at the southwestern point of the island (photo below) → **p. 95**

**INSIDERTIP** **Action-packed: guaranteed**

A full programme: the free @sun generation.com clubs offer fun activities for teens. With a full programme of outings and disco nights, not one second of their holiday will be boring → **p. 97**

**INSIDERTIP** **Adventure for water lovers**

In Le Waterpark & Leisure Village in Belle Mare, you can have fun splashing around and diving in the cool waters. Enjoy making full use of the wave pool and the high speed slides → **p. 98**

**INSIDERTIP** **A joyful celebration**

Divali is a Hindu festival that lasts several days and celebrates the victory of good over evil. Many houses are decorated with lights during the festivities → **p. 101**

# BEST OF ...

**FOR FREE**

● *Aapravasi Ghat*
Once upon a time this part of the harbour of Port Louis was a landing area and detention centre for immigrants arriving here to find work from the 19th century onwards. Although there are only a few remnants of the complex in existence today, the free tour gives an insight into the island's history → p. 47

● *The shell collector*
The poet Robert Edward Hart (1891–1954) lived in a small house on the picturesque south coast from 1941. The façade is completely covered with mussels and coral, something that would be forbidden today. Inside, they've preserved the poet's furniture and personal belongings. A quiet and peaceful place → p. 74

● *A view with music*
*Fort Adelaide* rises over Port Louis on top of the 100m/330ft-high Petite Montagne. Architecturally, the fortifications provide little of interest, but the view is fantastic and sometimes free concerts and other shows are also held in the inner courtyard → p. 49

● *Buried beneath the palm trees*
Opposite the island's oldest church is the *Pamplemousses Cemetery,* an enchanting place with many historic graves. The cemetery's occupants include Emmeline de Carcenac, known as Dame Creole, who was written about by Charles Baudelaire → p. 39

● *Pounding surf*
Gigantic waves break on the cliffs at the southern tip of the island. When it's windy, the elements perform an impressive spectacle here, which is why there's also a viewing platform at *Cap Gris Gris* → p. 73

● *A symphony in the pedestrian zone*
At weekends Mauritian bands come and play at the harbour and in the pedestrian zone of the *Caudan Waterfront Complex.* They start in the afternoon and carry on late into the evening. Everything's represented, from pop and jazz to sega and reggae (photo) → p. 53

●●●● Dots in guidebook refer to 'Best of ...' tips

### ● *On horseback*

Horse racing has been held on the *Champ de Mars* in Port Louis since 1812, making it the oldest racecourse in the southern hemisphere. However, you won't encounter signs of age or an atmosphere of snobbery here. Rather, you can enjoy the carnival atmosphere as all of Mauritius gathers to place their bets.
→ p. 48

### ● *Try on a sari*

*Goodlands* is the shopping city of the north and many shops line its main street. It's packed on market days when farmers and traders bring their goods to town. Indian fashions are sold as well as fruit, vegetables and spices. It's a dazzling explosion of colour → p. 38

### ● *Vegetables by bike*

Mauritians love snacks, and cheap filled pastries are sold everywhere, though there are usually only one or two varieties on offer. On the beach at *Grand Baie*, the sellers offer a veritable buffet of exotic snacks from a long row of stalls → p. 33

### ● *Dancing on the hot sand*

At weekends, Mauritian families meet on the public beaches to have a picnic. They usually come to the beach loaded with pre-cooked food. The festive atmosphere grows steadily as people begin to play and dance to traditional Sega music. A real experience (photo) → p. 35

### ● *Forget the aquarium – visit the harbour*

Fish is expensive on Mauritius. If you want to buy it cheaply, wait for the fishermen at the harbour. Most harbours have fish landing stations where they sell the previous night's catch around midday. Above all, however, when you come here, you'll get an impression of the Indian Ocean's marvellous, colourful fauna → p. 33

### ● *Family visits in the New Year*

Only a very few Mauritians work in the first week of January and many businesses are closed. It's also a time when families travel everywhere on the island with their children, either to visit relatives, or to observe the tradition of getting new clothes at this time of year. It can almost seem like a mass exodus of people is taking place → p. 100

ONLY IN

# BEST OF ...

RAIN

● *Walk under the water!*
Go for a walk on the bottom of the sea! This experience is offered on the north coast around Grand Baie. Wearing a helmet with a supply of air pumped in, you're free to go for a walk! (photo) → p. 35

● *The Museum of Natural History*
The era of the dodo, a flightless bird found only on Mauritius, ended in 1690 when sailors took the last of the species onto their ships as provisions. The *Natural History Museum* shows a reconstruction of the animal, along with exhibitions about the island's flora and fauna → p. 50

● *Cookies from an old recipe*
In the Ville Noir of Mahébourg, the Raults family have been making cookies from the cassava root based on a family recipe since 1870. Visit the bake house and try them for yourself! → p. 64

● *A legendary postage stamp*
The *Blue Mauritius* postage stamp is one of the Mauritian people's most treasured possessions. For this reason it spends most of the day in darkness in the Blue Penny Museum. Make sure to ask about a guided tour, during which they'll turn on the lights → p. 48

● *Shop 'til you drop*
While most shopping centres are geared to a more local audience, the selection of goods on offer in the *Cascavelle Shopping Village* is attractive to holiday makers as well. Around 60 shops and many restaurants can be found in this complex, situated outside Flic en Flac → p. 81

● *Clothes galore*
Mauritius exports textiles around the world. Much of them end up, however, in the *Quatre Bornes Clothes Market*. When it's raining, you can have a good rummage around and try things on under the shelter of tarpaulins → p. 82

# RELAX AND CHILL OUT
## Take it easy and spoil yourself

● *An island of bliss*
Let's be honest: people fly to Mauritius for relaxation and recuperation. Everything's geared to this aim in the island's beach hotels. But even away from these carefully managed resorts, you can find cosy and, above all, secluded spots. Take a walk on *Île aux Cerfs* and watch the sun set → p. 67

● *Take a look at the boats*
Just a few steps away from the shore, you can sit on the terrace of the *Beach House* in Grand Baie and look out at the yachts bobbing on the water with a cocktail in your hand. It doesn't get much better than this → p. 36

● *Wine beneath a waterfall*
Pack your beach towels, some wine and a selection of snacks (many are sold all along the roadside). Then have someone show you the way from Souillac to the *Rochester Falls* and spread out your picnic in the waterfall's tranquil surroundings → p. 74

● *The scent of carefree living*
The *spa at the Hotel Dinarobin* is located at the foot of the Morne Brabant mountain. Two of the eight massage rooms are out in the open air, surrounded by lush, tropical vegetation. Let the delicate scents wash over you and enjoy the soothing treatments → p. 72

● *Tranquillity at the lily pond*
In the *Botanical Garden* at Pamplemousses there are lots of beautiful places to stop and linger a while, which is why pairs of young lovers are drawn here. You'll really miss out if you walk through the park without a guide, because they have an inexhaustible knowledge of the garden's plant life → p. 38

● *A study in serenity*
On some public holidays, up to 300,000 worshippers come to *Grand Bassin*. Otherwise, it's not unusual to have the entire pavilion, which looks out over the lake, all to yourself. You'll get a view of the temple complex and the enormous statue of Shiva (photo) → p. 70

# INTRODUCTION

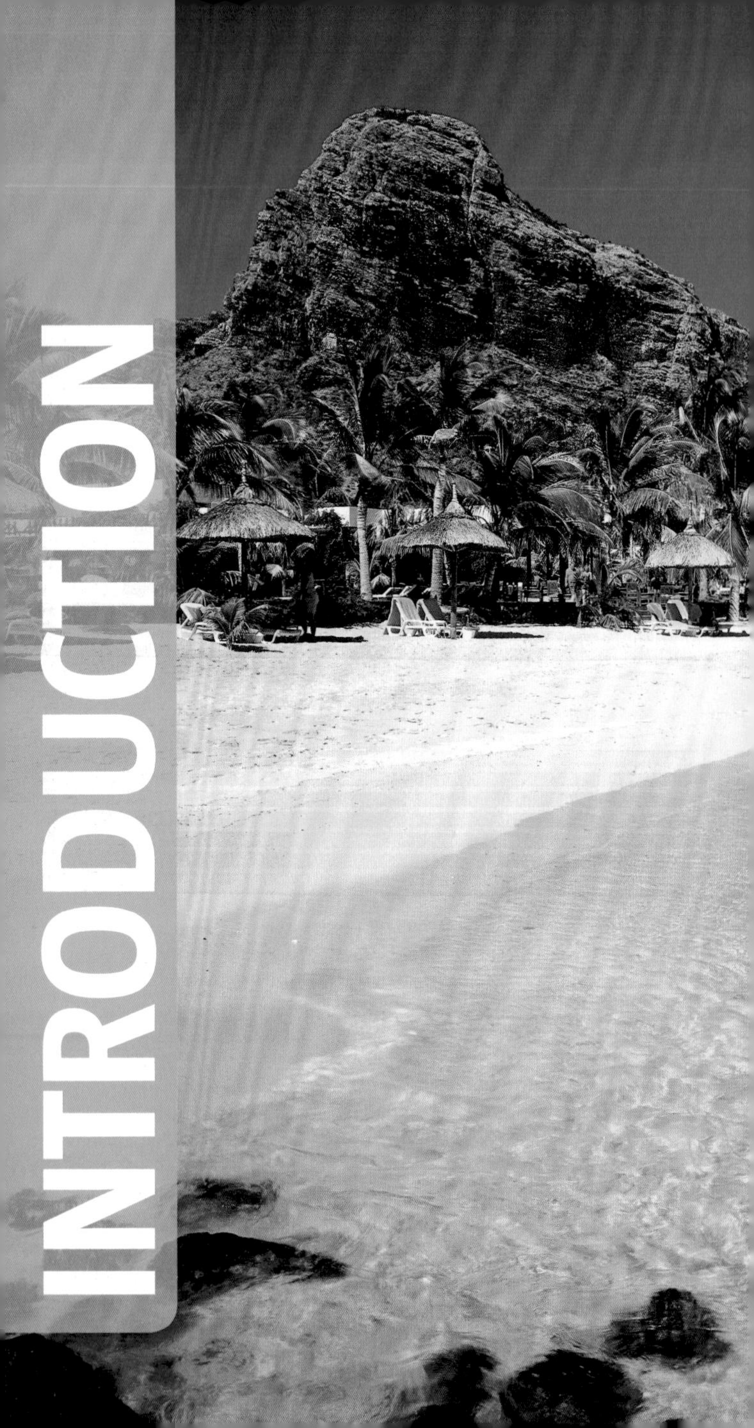

# DISCOVER MAURITIUS!

When people fly to Mauritius, they're usually looking for sunshine and beautiful beaches. Their every wish is granted in this charming corner of the world whose small area is home to a constantly changing topographical and cultural landscape. Travelling from the beach to the rainforest takes only an hour, and Tamil temples are only five minutes away from Christian shrines. In the capital of Port Louis, hustle and bustle reigns during the day, but you don't have to go very far to find colourful villages that seem to come from a time long past. What's more, everywhere you go the Mauritians will give you the warmest of welcomes. Mark Twain once said that God first created Mauritius, and then used it as the blueprint for paradise.

In the tour operators' glossy brochures, Mauritius is often called the 'Diamond of the Indian Ocean'. The island is a fabulous destination for sun worshippers who expect a certain standard whether in terms of accommodation, food or service. Sun, palms, white sandy beaches, sea water that's invitingly warm for swimming, turquoise bays, and attractive resorts with large swimming pools – all of this and much more besides

Photo: The beach of Le Paradis Hotel in Le Morne Brabant

is promised (and delivered!) by this island situated in the tropics and located in the middle of the world's warmest ocean.

Only 25 years ago Mauritius was considered a luxury, exclusive holiday resort that was only open to a privileged few. Indeed, the luxury hotels with their legendary service, sublime wellness facilities, and spacious golf courses are still among the best in the world. If you're looking for something special, you won't be disappointed. Today, however, almost all tourist operators offer the island in their brochures and provide good, value-for-money alternatives to the top hotels, and a stay next to the Indian Ocean certainly doesn't have to be expensive. Sun worshippers will be just as happy here as activity lovers and sports fans. All kinds of people come here, from globetrotters to film stars, and there's something on offer to meet every desire. Although the number of visitors is steadily increasing and more and more hotels are spreading out along the beaches, this remote island has retained its magical charm.

One facet of the diverse culture: the Hindus' colourful garments.

> **Sun worshippers will feel just as at home here as activity seekers**

In the 16th century when Portuguese sailors discovered the island which, with an area of 1,865 km²/1160mi² is not much larger than London, they found only a few species of birds, a tropical jungle, and a large lagoon lined with a coral reef. After unsuccessful colonisation attempts by the Dutch, whose lives were made difficult by tropical storms and pirates, the French settled here, bringing with them slaves from Africa and Madagascar. At the start of the 19th century the British captured the colony and enticed more than one million Indian contract labourers to the

around 900
Mauritius is already known to Arab seafarers

1511
The Portuguese seafarer Pedro Mascarenhas discovers the uninhabited island.

1598
The Dutch take over the island and name it after their head of state, Prince Moritz (Maurice) of Nassau.

1710
The Dutch leave and pirates settle on the island.

1715
Mauritius is occupied by the French

country. Chinese specialist workers were also added to this total. No wonder, then, that the population of today's Republic of Mauritius is composed of many ethnic groups. People of all skin colours get on well with each other, however, and tolerate their different customs and religions. They're proud of their island and its cultural diversity. Créole, the unofficial language spoken every day by almost all of

**A coral reef surrounds nearly the whole island**

the 1.2 million inhabitants, also plays an important part in building their national identity.

The varied landscape of this tropical island is as diverse as its population. Mauritius was formed by volcanic eruptions in the sea around seven or eight million years ago. The cones of these long-extinct, fiery mountains still rise high into the sky. The gradual sinking of the lava floor formed the coral reefs. This reef runs around almost the entire island and acts as a boundary to the peaceful lagoons where the water's never deeper than 4m. With a temperature of 24–27°C/75–80°F, the island's calm

Mauritius is a paradise for diving and snorkelling fans

**1735**
Mahé de Labourdonnais founds Port Louis, the capital and a port town

**1748–1810**
The English repeatedly try to take the island

**2nd December 1810**
The French surrender in Port Napoléon (now Port Louis)

**1814**
The French and English divide up their spoils: La Réunion stays in French hands; Mauritius, Rodrigues and the Seychelles, however, go to England. 78,000 people live on Mauritius, 80 per cent of whom are slaves

**12 | 13**

waters offer virtually unlimited swimming possibilities and excellent conditions for water sports fans. High waves and sharks are held at bay by the reef, and the large fish beyond the coral belt have become prized hunting quarry for enthusiastic anglers. Throughout the year the air temperature is between 24–30°C/75–80°F and the sun pampers the green island, meaning that its unique vegetation can thrive.

## Tourism has changed the face of the island

Despite this tropical greenhouse climate, when it gained its independence Mauritius found it difficult to feed itself without the help of a colonial power. At one point the government tried to find an alternative to sugar cane, which is grown on 80 per cent of the useable agricultural surface of the island. It created a free trade zone in 1970 and lured in investors, who predominantly came from the textile industry and began to produce fashionable clothing here. This industry survives to the present day. At the same time, the tourist market was developed and the island was marketed well.

Tourism has changed the face of the island, but its charm remains unaffected. More and more hotels are opening their doors along the most beautiful stretches of beach, and peaceful fishing villages have given way to holiday resorts. Although this development has not brought benefits to all of the Mauritian people, they are nevertheless very friendly towards foreigners.

The future of the island's economic development, and above all the sugar industry, is uncertain. The Mauritian government is trying, through the diversification of its industrial and agricultural production, to meet the challenges of the 21st century, and is strengthening its efforts in the IT sector in particular. Evidence of this can be seen in *Cybercity, the* high-tech industrial zone in Port Louis. Glittering skyscrapers and fancy hotels cannot hide the fact, however, that Mauritius is heavily dependent on the global economy and the European market in particular. Despite all the advantages of modern life, social security and unemployment benefits are still foreign concepts on the island, and the majority of the population can only dream of the type of lifestyle that's presented to them in advertisements. Many people have tried setting up small businesses, and have started offering services or renting a couple of rooms or apartments to tourists. By such means they're trying to get a share of the

**1835**
The abolition of slavery; workers are brought to the island from India and China

**1854–99**
The number of inhabitants is halved due to epidemics and natural disasters

**1958**
Universal suffrage is introduced

**1968**
Mauritius becomes a sovereign state of the British Commonwealth

**1992**
Declaration of the Republic

**2008**
Morne Brabant becomes a Unesco World Heritage Site

world's wealth for themselves. This flourishing of small businesses means that it's now very easy to find a place to stay without arranging ahead. Without a hotel booked on arrival, however, you won't get an entry visa.

Mauritius offers much more than just beach holidays. It's worth going on a voyage of discovery in a rented car or getting to meet the local people first hand on a journey by bus. But it's by bike or on foot that you can get closest to the island's smaller beauties. Travelling in this way you'll get to breathe in the scent of the bougainvillea, feel the salty sea breeze on your skin, hear the wind rustling through the sugar cane,

Religion is an important part of Mauritian life: the pagoda in Port Louis

and listen to the song of the island's tropical birds. In remote river valleys and on the tops of mountains, you can discover the diversity of the native flora. In the deepest thickets of the ancient rainforests you can also find the last remnants of the once species-rich bird life of the island, including the extremely rare Mauritius kestrel and the picture perfect pink pigeon. More often, however, you'll see species introduced by humans, such as the Javanese deer, monkeys and wild pigs. A lush, perpetual bloom grows in the gardens here, and a colourful underwater flora and

**Rare birds live deep in the jungle**

fauna flourish in the coral reef and around many of the surrounding islands. If you travel with your eyes peeled and your ears open, you'll discover everything Mauritius has to offer.

# WHAT'S HOT

## 1 Two's company

*Wellness.* The island's spas have discovered romance. In the *Four Seasons Mauritius at Anahita (Beau Champ)* they don't just offer heavenly massages, but also courses that teach you how to give magical massages yourself. It's said that pleasure is always doubled if it's shared. The spa professionals at the *Maradiva Villas Resort & Spa (Wolmar)* know this well. Here, you and your loved one can receive treatments at the same time. The Couple's Suite at the *Heritage Le Telfair (Domaine de Bel Ombre, see photo)* is also luxurious, and comes with a private pool.

## Seggae in your veins 2

*Music.* The seggae sound is a combination of Caribbean reggae and Mauritian sega. Seggae gets both your ears and your feet involved. Musicians like Azaria Topize and his band Salawi, or the six-member combo, the *Otentikk Street Brothers (www.osbcrew.com)* can regularly be seen live. A glance at the daily newspapers or at posters will reveal what's going on. Michael Lascar is a seggae musician who's achieved international success well beyond the confines of Mauritius *(www.michael-lascar.ch)*.

## 3 Head into the wind

*Kitesurfing.* When the wind is still too weak for surfing, the kitesurfers are already on their boards. With a sail in the wind and a surfboard under their feet, experienced kitesurfers criss-cross their way outside Manawa or Chameaux. If you've yet to get into extreme sports, you should visit the lagoon at the *Hotel Paladien Marina*. There, the usually light onshore winds make wipeouts impossible, and the trainers of *Kitezone (Coastal Road, Anse La Raie, Photo)* will explain how to handle the equipment. *Kitesurf Paradise (near Hotel La Palmeraie, Belle Mare)* and *Air Switch (Le Morne)* also offer courses.

# An underwater world

**Diving experiences.** There are lots of artists in Mauritius, but an underwater painter is something extraordinary. Jean-Michel Langlois dives out of burning curiosity and lets his creativity run wild with waterproof painting materials. The resulting works of art make great souvenirs *(Blues Diving Center at the Hotel Belle Mare Plage, Belle Mare)*. Lots of companies now offer trips in submarines. For something a little more special, take a ride in *Blue Safari (www.blue-safari.com)*. This trip lets you dive down in a luxurious submarine and eat lunch followed by dessert and coffee at a depth of nearly 35m below the surface. If you prefer getting your feet wet, go to the *Tamarino Ocean Pro* Diving School *(Tamarin Bay, photo)*. Professional divers can show you the best diving spots on the island's west coast. They also know the underwater caves and hot water vents like the back of their hand.

# A good combination

**Culinary delights.** Mauritius is a veritable melting pot, something that also shows in their cooking. Contemporary influences from around the world, local ingredients and historical connections will all be apparent on your plate. For example, the picturesque *Domaine Anna (Flic en Flac, photo)* is a crossroads for Mauritian and French cuisine. Whether you're eating shrimps in a coriander and lime sauce, squid with saffron or flambéed rum banana, in the *Hidden Reef Restaurant (Royal Road, Pointe aux Canonniers)* all the points of the compass complement each other in delicious combinations. The vanilla chicken from *Le Saint Aubin (Rivière des Anguilles)* sounds unusual, but it's definitely worth a try!

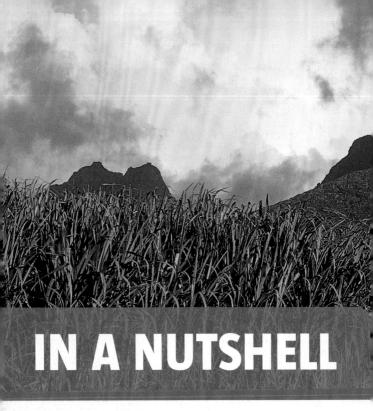

# IN A NUTSHELL

## BLUE MARLIN
A relatively short way beyond the coral reef, the sea around Mauritius becomes very deep, thus making it ideal fishing grounds for deep-sea anglers. The most commonly hunted fish is the blue marlin, which here often weighs more than 500kg/1,100lb. The high season begins in November and ends in March. You can find all the necessary equipment everywhere along the coast.

## BLUE MAURITIUS
An error resulted in the 'Orange Mauritius' and 'Blue Mauritius' postage stamps, printed in 1847, becoming extremely rare valuable collectibles that have gained fame around the world. Mauritius was the first colony to issue postage stamps (the very first were issued in Britain in 1840). The engraver Joseph Barnard engraved the words 'Post Office' next to a picture of the British Queen Victoria on a copper plate and printed 500 copies. Lady Gomm, the wife of the then British governor of Mauritius, adorned 150 of 350 invitations to a ball with these new stamps. Shortly after, it was realised that he should have marked the stamps with the inscription 'Post Paid' instead. Today, there are 13 orange-coloured One Penny stamps and 12 blue Two Penny stamps known to be in existence. In 1993 a Mauritian syndicate bought a copy of each for a total of 1.2 million £/2 million $. The precious originals are on display in the Blue Penny Museum in Port Louis.

Photo: Sugar cane fields

Tragic Roman heroes, exciting music, exotic plants and amazing animals – the nature and culture of Mauritius are dazzling

# COLONIAL VILLAS

Unfortunately only a few of the elegant country houses built on the island by rich families at the start of the 19th century remain today. Exotic woods were used as building materials and a covered veranda usually went right round the house, leading to the doors of each room. This allowed such good ventilation that the heat remained bearable even in the height of summer. To reduce the risk of fire, the kitchens were located in separate stone buildings. An impression of these houses' former glory is conveyed by the residences *Eureka* (1838) in Moka and the *Domaine des Aubineaux* at Curepipe, both of which have been turned into museums. Eureka is fitted out with valuable furniture from the 19th century. In Les Aubineaux, you can get a sense of the artistic intentions of the former owner, Louis-Myriam Harel, who died in 1999. Built from stone, the administrative and *representative buildings* from the colonial era have been less affected by fires and cyclones and have been preserved in large numbers. Examples are the *Naval Museum* in Mahébourg, the *Collège Royal* in Curepipe, and Government House, the *Mauritius Institute* and the *Theatre* in Port Louis. However, they lack the lightness and playfulness of the gleaming white private residences.

it arrives. When this happens, it's essential to secure all possessions and to stock up on supplies. People who live in sheet metal huts take shelter in public buildings. It only takes a few hours for a cyclone to cross the island, but it usually leaves behind such an image of horror

Eureka – one of the best preserved colonial villas in Mauritius

# CYCLONES

Cyclones are whirlwinds that can occur between December and April. They are formed over the sea near the equator when the water is heated above 26°C/79°F for a long time and thus evaporates very quickly. Near the centre of a cyclone the storm reaches speeds of 250km/155mi per hour, causing flash floods and massive levels of precipitation. On land the storms have catastrophic effects: streets are flooded, huts are blown away, trees are uprooted and plants are ripped out of the fields. A coming storm is broadcast in all languages in the Mauritian media several days before

that it looks as if it had been raging for days.

# DODO

This bird, which became extinct in the 17th century, is more present today than ever. Replicas in all conceivable shapes and sizes, including stuffed animals and pictures emblazoned on coffee mugs, are available in the souvenir shops. Restaurants and bars are named after the dodo and it's been officially honoured as the island's national emblem.

The dodo (Raphus cucullatus), which belonged to the family of pigeons, was a little larger than a turkey. It had small legs, a heavy, extremely plump body, a round head with a featherless face, a long neck and a big, hooked beak. Instead of wings, the dodo had short stumps, and instead of a tail it had a fine brush of feathers. It couldn't fly and hatched its eggs on the ground, both becoming reasons for its undoing. Although dodo meat was said not to have been particularly tasty, the early Dutch sailors appreciated the bird as it added a bit of variety to their rather monotonous diet on board ship during voyages. It's also reported that sailors killed the bird just for the sheer fun of it. It's more likely, however, that the bird's demise was due largely to the animals introduced to the island by man, including rats, pigs, goats and monkeys. You can see a reconstruction of a dodo on display in the Natural History Museum in Port Louis.

## FILAOS

It's not coconut palms that line the white sandy beaches of Mauritius, as the stereotype of the tropics would have it, but filaos, also called casuarinas. These trees were introduced from Australia in the 18th century. As with the coconut palm, Filaos also like growing in the slightly salty ground of the beach. The reason for its rapid spread, however, is that the tree's trunks and branches are flexible enough to bend and give way during severe hurricanes and cyclones. Their appearance recalls that of the European larch, but in fact the 'needles' are extensions of branches which look similar to horsetails when they are put together.

## LANGUAGES

The administrative language is English, the upper classes speak French, and Mauritians use Creole amongst themselves in their everyday lives. Hindi, Urdu, Marathi, Telegu and Cantonese are minority languages, but are also taught in schools. The only tongue that the authorities continue to ignore is Creole, a language that's spoken by 95 per cent of Mauritians. The vocabulary of Creole is based on French and is peppered with Madagascan, Indian and English elements. The media broadcasts advertisements and a daily news bulletin in the Creole language, but French dominates at all other times. Indian movies are shown in the Hindi original. As a visitor to the island you can get by speaking English, but Mauritians prefer to speak French.

## MAHÉ DE LABOURDONNAIS

Bertrand François Mahé de Labourdonnais was born in Saint-Malo in 1699. Initially working for the merchant navy, he became Governor General of the Mascarene Islands in 1735 and, while in this position, secured French rule of the Indian Ocean. He founded the city of Port Louis, expanded the harbour, created a network of roads, built Government House and established the first large sugar mill and fortresses to defend the Island. He lost his position ten years later through plots and intrigue and spent several years in prison in France. Although his reputation was restored, he died in 1753, broken and impoverished. Through his commitment and vision, he laid the foundation stone for the development of the island.

## NATIONAL FLOWER

Trochetia Boutoniana, known as 'boucle d'oreille' (earring) in Creole, only grows on the slopes of Morne Brabant. The orange-coloured nectar of the plant's bright red flowers smells like vanilla. This attracts geckos, bees and birds. The Trochetia Boutoniana has been the national flower of Mauritius since 1994.

# PAUL AND VIRGINIE

With his novel 'Paul et Virginie', the Frenchman Jacques-Henri Bernardin de Saint-Pierre (1737-1814) created a monument not only to love, but also to the tropical jungle of Mauritius. Two children of nature grow up in a remote valley. They are playmates at first, and later discover their love for each other. Virginie, however, is sent to France. Dying with longing for Paul, she embarks on the St Géran to Mauritius, but the boat is wrecked on a reef off the island. The girl drowns in the waves in front of Paul, who's following the drama from the shore. Paul eventually dies from a broken heart. As though the two had actually lived in reality, you can follow the traces of the pair all over the island. Monuments have been dedicated to them in Port Louis and in Curepipe; it's claimed that Virginie and her mother regularly visited the church in Pamplemousses; and you can even find the girl's 'grave' in the Botanical Garden. There's also a monument in Poudre d'Or to the misfortune of the ship 'St Géran', which was actually wrecked on 17 April 1744 near Île d'Ambre; parts of the wreck are on display in the museum at Mahébourg. Restaurants and hotels are named after Paul and Virginie, and you can buy the book's illustrations in the form of valuable old engravings and printed on T-shirts. The novel, published in 1788, has been translated into 30 languages.

# ROUTE ROYALE

In every town and village in Mauritius the main street is always called Route Royale. This is occasionally translated as Royal Street, but more often as Royal Road. Quite often, all three variants are used in one town. Shops, restaurants and bars are located on these streets. Since there are no house numbers on Mauritius, the addresses of all major businesses are identical. For foreigners, this either means that you must keep an attentive eye out when driving up and down streets, or you must ask a local. However, since even locals often don't know the names of the side streets themselves, you'll often only learn the name of a business in the immediate neighbourhood. Contrary to appearances, the Route Royale isn't a continuous street that crosses the whole island, an impression that creeps up on you particularly quickly when travelling along the northwest coast.

# SEEWOOSAGUR RAMGOOLAM

The name Seewoosagur Ramgoolam is encountered all over Mauritius. The airport, the Botanical Garden, the largest hospital and many other institutions carry the name. There's also a street that bears the name in almost every village and town. Ramgoolam was born in Mauritius in 1900, the son of Indian parents. After studying medicine in Britain, he returned to his homeland, and very soon after began fighting for the, at first modest, autonomy of the island. From 1948 he was chairman of the Labour Party campaigning for Mauritian independence. This goal was achieved in 1968 and Ramgoolam became the island's first Prime Minister. His reign lasted until 1982. After his party lost its majority he held the office of Governor General, a ceremonial position with few actual powers. Ramgoolam died in 1985. He's known in Mauritius as the 'Father of the Nation and the Architect of Independence'.

## SEGA

Sega is a music of African origin that was developed by slaves at the end of the 18th century, perhaps to sing during their work in the fields, and also possibly for pleasure during the little spare time they had. Until the 1980s, hardly anyone outside the Creole population took it seriously. Today, however, it's considered an important part of Mauritian culture. Every major hotel organises sega evenings. Although the authenticity of these colourful events is doubtful, they do have their charm. The songs of sega deal with love and everyday life, but they also take an ironic look at the current political problems of the day. The associated dance, performed by several women and one man, is an expression of pure eroticism. Originally, the songs were played with simple instruments: a triangle, a maravane (a box filled with grains), the bobre (a steel string stretched over a gourd) and the ravanne (a flat drum). In modern sega, sometimes derisively known as 'séga-salon', the musicians also use an accordion and an electric guitar. For some time now, Indian artists have also drawn inspiration from this music. Creole people sometimes try to combine the rhythms of sega with those of reggae, and use their pieces for making political statements. They call this music ‹seggae›.

## SUGAR CANE

It's said that the island of Mauritius has two landscapes: one seen before and one after the sugar cane harvest. If you drive through the country from March to June, the tall plants sometimes rise up like walls at either side of the road. Eighty per cent of the island's agricultural land is cultivated with sugar cane. Visitors can learn how juice is extracted from the stems of the plant and pro-

cessed into sugar in several locations: in a reconstructed old factory in the *Domaine Les Pailles* leisure centre; in *L'Aventure du Sucre*, a new, very informative sugar museum near Pamplemouss-

Fancy a chat? Most people in Mauritius understand English

es; or on modern farms where there's usually someone set aside and given the task of showing guests around the plant. The island's sugar industry is currently in a state of upheaval. For a long time an agreement with the EU secured the producers prices that were significantly above world market levels. This privilege will, however, run out in 2015. In the future, the sugar producers therefore want to earn more from processing the by-products of sugar refinery, molasses and bagasse, into bio fuels. The energy production from bagasse alone is expected to double to 600 gigawatts by 2015.

# FOOD & DRINK

If you're not staying the night in Grand Baie, Péreybère or in the centre of Flic en Flac, you'd do well to book half-board accommodation because restaurants are difficult to reach from most holiday resort hotels.

If you choose a self-catering apartment or a guesthouse near a town, however, you'll have the choice between snack bars, street stalls, eateries, pizzerias and gourmet restaurants. As hygiene conditions are generally good, even sensitive stomachs shouldn't have a problem. It would be a shame, therefore, never to eat outside your hotel. Hardly anywhere else in the world is the range of Indian, Creole, Chinese and French dishes on offer greater than it is here. Particularly in the top restaurants and luxury hotels,

the chefs create extravagant delicacies from three continents. You shouldn't expect too much of the facilities or the service in the eateries beyond the tourist centres. The exotic cuisine and the friendliness of the staff make up for any deficiencies, however.

Along the streets the restaurants are primarily Creole, Chinese, European and Indian. Japanese and Thai cuisine and wild game dishes are occasionally offered. Vegetarians will particularly appreciate the variety of foods offered by Indian restaurants. The buffets in the hotels have a different theme every night, and sometimes there's also a choice of menu. If you choose to eat in one of the hotel's main speciality restaurants instead, you'll normally get a discount. These restau-

A mix of Mauritian and international cuisine – enjoy this great culinary fusion in gourmet restaurants or from roadside stalls.

rants usually offer Mediterranean cuisine, wild game, barbecues, seafood or French haute cuisine. Bear in mind that restaurants can be expensive as there's not enough volume all year round to allow economies of scale, and wine is largely over-priced due to severe import duties. But it's still better to eat in restaurants compared with hotels, especially if you intend to have wine. Most restaurants are open for lunch from noon to 2pm and in the evening from 6pm; it's difficult to find anything open after 9.30pm.

Regardless of whether a Mauritian has Indian-Hindu or Muslim roots, or is of Chinese, French or Creole descent, everyone on the island shares the best of each other's cuisine, while always taking care to adhere to the habits and customs of their own culture. A Hindu will prepare *biryani* without beef, for instance, substituting it with lamb or chicken instead, and Muslims will avoid a Chinese pork dish. The Creole people are the least

# LOCAL SPECIALITIES

▶ **alouda** – a milk-like drink that's available in a pink, light green or yellow vanilla variety. It's good served chilled with fruit seeds and jelly pieces

▶ **boulettes chinoises** – small dough balls that are deep-fried and served as snacks

▶ **biryani** – a spicy rice dish with pieces of meat, eggs and vegetables

▶ **cabri massalé** – goat's meat in a spicy masala sauce, a popular speciality that's eaten after Hindu sacrificial ceremonies

▶ **cari de cerf** – venison stew in a hearty tomato and onion sauce

▶ **cari or curry de poulet** – chicken, tomatoes, onions and masala powder cooked together and served with rice and pulses

▶ **curry d'agneau avec coco et raisins** – mild lamb curry, flavoured with coconut sauce and raisins (photo left)

▶ **gâteau patate** – a succulent, firm cake made from sweet potatoes. It's the national dessert of Mauritius

▶ **mine frite** – a Creole variation on a Chinese noodle dish, available with a choice of chicken, beef or fish

▶ **ourite sauce piquante** – a speciality made from fresh or dried squid. It's cooked in a sauce flavoured with turmeric (curcuma), chilli and ginger

▶ **poisson sauce créole** – a whole grilled fish or a fish fillet served in a spicy tomato sauce

▶ **punch** – punch, particularly home-made, is served as an aperitif. The stronger variety of rhum arrangé (rum with added herbs) is also recommended as an after-dinner drink

▶ **rougaille de bœuf** – a kind of beef stew in a sauce flavoured with coriander (*cotomili*)

▶ **samoussas** – pastries fried in oil until crispy, with various savoury fillings

prejudiced about taking culinary inspiration from everywhere. Their everyday foods are called *cari (curry)*, *daube* and *rougaille*. These are meat, poultry and fish dishes with different sauces, all of which are served with rice, lentils and beans *(grains)*, or brèdes (steamed vegetable leaves) and *chatini*, a freshly prepared mixture of raw tomatoes and chilli. To make the sauces, *pommes d'amour* (literally 'love apples', the Mauritian name for tomatoes), onions, masala and turmeric powder, as well as coriander *(cotomili)*, chilli and spicy *cari poulet* leaves are all integral ingredients. *Vindaye* is a dish made from pieces of meat or fish simmered in a sauce made of ginger, garlic, onions and vinegar. The Indian custom of adding flatbreads *(rotis, nans* or *faratas)* to a meal finds followers throughout the island, but sometimes you'll also get a baguette.

If you're on an island tour, you should visit one of the simple, affordable 'snacks' (snack bars) and try cooked or fried noodles (mine bouille or mine frite). You should also taste the spicy snacks that are sold from stalls or from bicycle stands. In most cases, these consist of deep-fried pastries *(samoussas)* that are filled with meat or vegetables. They only cost a few rupees and are served wrapped in newspaper. *Dholl pouris* is a type of flatbread with yellow split peas. Breads made from white or brown flour are all collectively known as *farathas*. Under no circumstance should you miss sampling from the large variety of fantastic fresh fruits.

## DRINK

There are three varieties of beer brewed on Mauritius: *Phoenix* and *Black Eagle* are similar to pale lagers, and *Blue Marlin* could be classified as a 'weak stout'. The wine produced on the island (referred to as *local wine*) is produced and fermented from imported varieties of grape. The South African wine sold on Mauritius is very good, and there's usually a large selection on restaurants' drinks menus. Beer, like rum, is available at kiosks everywhere and is also drunk on the roadside. The cocktails and rum-based mixed drinks *(punchs)* that are available at hotel bars are absolutely delicious. Freshly squeezed juices and cocktails made from exotic fruits are vita-

Exotic soul food: Creole dishes

min-rich and very tasty. You should definitely try *lassi* (a yoghurt drink) and drinkable coconut milk at least once during your visit. A drink made from lemongrass is a very refreshing choice in the heat of the day: the leaves are boiled briefly in water; the brew is then cooled and sweetened with sugar syrup.

# SHOPPING

Nothing can escape the dodo on Mauritius; the extinct bird's to be found in every souvenir shop. However, the island doesn't just offer tacky trinkets. The Government has worked hard to promote additional economic revenue streams in addition to sugar cane cultivation and tourism. The most important are the textile and jewellery industries, as well as the making of model ships.

## DRINKS

Mauritian tea is sold in supermarkets as a black blend or flavoured with vanilla or coconut. Rum has greatly improved in recent years. The most famous brand is *Green Island*; the *Saint Aubin* domain also sells good rum that is pure or flavoured with vanilla or coffee. In the *Rhumerie Chamarel* you can buy white sugar cane liquors and a type of alcohol that's distilled like cognac.

## FLOWERS

The heart-shaped anthurium (a.k.a. the 'flamingo flower') is a popular souvenir. You can order them by phone at *Sun Souvenir* (tel. 6373784). You'll receive your bouquet at the airport, packed and ready to fly.

## JEWELLERY

There aren't any diamonds on Mauritius, but imported gems are polished here. Some factories have showrooms selling jewellery for duty-free export. The most famous diamond workshops and jewellers are *Adamas, Caunhye Bijoux* and *Poncini*, which have branches in hotels and shopping centres. Goldsmith Bernd Wilhelm also makes designer jewellery at his workshop in Quatre Bornes. You should ring ahead before visiting *(B. W. Necklaces Ltd. | tel. 4 67 94 75 | www. berndwilhelm.com)*.

## MARKETS

You can buy things cheaply at the markets, where you can see fruit and vegetables sold next to clothes, fabrics, baskets and crockery. Haggling isn't normal with food, but all other prices are up for discussion.

Markets: *Abercrombie (Tue/Sun/Sat); Centre de Flacq (Wed/Sun); Curepipe (Wed/Sat); Goodlands (Tue/Fri); Mahébourg (Mon); Port Louis (Daily); Quatre Bornes (Thu/Sun clothes market; Wed/ Sat exclusively a vegetable market)*

# Rum, model ships, textiles and jewellery: tourists can benefit from buying direct from the factories on the island

## MODEL SHIPS

The quality of these small-scale models made according to historical blueprints is very high. Nevertheless, the prices are very low: they start at 2000 rupees and you can get really excellent pieces for 12,000 rupees. There are lots of historical ships to choose from, but the factories are also happy to make other models based on customers' own designs. The most comprehensive range can be found in the *Historic Marine* factory *(Zone Industrielle de St. Antoine | Goodlands | Mon–Fri 8.30am–5pm, Sat/Sun 9am–noon | tel. 2 83 93 04 | www.historic-marine.com)*.

## SHOPPING CENTRES

The best range can be found in Grand Baie at the *Sunset Boulevard*. The promenade's shops mainly offer sport and leisure fashion for tourists. Prices are similar to those in Europe. The most popular shopping centres include the *Orchard Centre* on St Jean Road in Quatre Bornes, the *Trianon Shopping Centre* (on the motorway), the *Cascavelle Shopping Mall* on the road to Flic en Flac, the Arcades Curimjee in Curepipe and the *Galleries Evershine* in Rose Hill. The *Caudan* and the Port Louis Waterfront at *Port Louis'* old harbour are the most beautiful. All big companies have branches there. There are also elegant boutiques in *Happy World House*.

## TEXTILES

Textile factories on the island make mass-produced goods and elegant suits. Seconds and surplus goods are sold in the factory shops: T-shirts and sweaters can be found in the *Knitwear-Boutique* in Floréal, and off-the-peg garments are for sale at Corona Clothing in Curepipe. Premium items can be found at the Caudan Waterfront *(www.caudan.com)* in Port Louis. Maille Street and Harris Wilson in the capital sell cashmere and fine knitwear.

# THE PERFECT ROUTE

## FAR FROM THE MADDING CROWD

You'll need a whole day for this car tour that goes once round the whole island. Since it would take an age to get through the traffic jams in the centre of Port Louis, the route begins to the south of the capital city and ends on its northern edge. You can also start at any point on the route, or stop at any moment and take a trip through the island's interior.

### ORIGINAL MAURITIUS

The beaches at the beginning of the route are hardly touched by tourism and the biggest attraction in some of the places you pass through is the supermarket. However, the region also gives an impression of how Mauritius looked once upon a time. ① *Flic en Flac* → p. 80 will meet the demands of tourists looking to party, but you should still break up your trip by taking a walk in ② *Casela Nature & Leisure Park* → p. 84

### BETWEEN HIGHLANDS AND LOWLANDS

On the west coast sea salt is obtained in shallow pools all along the road. At ③ *Tamarin* → p. 83, the best-known surfing location on the island, the flat plains are overlooked by the Tourelle du Tamarin (photo left). Conversely, the sea in front of ④ *Grande Rivière Noire* → p. 71 is very deep, meaning that the harbour is a centre for deep-sea anglers. The slopes of the Black River Gorges National Park rise up on the east of the road and the steep cliffs of the ⑤ *Morne Brabant* → p. 72 soon emerge out of the sea. Then the coast becomes wilder. The poet *Robert Edward Hart* once resided here and today his house is a ⑥ *Museum* → p. 74. The route continues, running past sugar cane fields and through predominantly Muslim villages where the women are sometimes veiled.

### DANGEROUS SURF

Beyond ⑦ *Mahébourg* → p. 62, the route travels through the most beautiful area on the island from the jungle to the sea to the north. It's worth making a stop in ⑧ *Kestrel Valley* → p. 65. However, take care: don't forget the time! The flat plains extend around ⑨ *Centre de Flacq* → p. 61. This region is predominantly home to a Hindu population. On a headland they've built the Temple of ⑩ *Sagar Shir Mandir* → p. 61 that looks as though it's floating above the sea. The beaches become ever more picturesque as you travel on. There aren't any villages here, but there are a few villas and luxury hotels. The fact that the sea here can

make navigating ships difficult is reflected in the name of the ⑪ *Cap Malheureux* → p. 40. The view of the islands makes this part of the route very charming indeed.

## FROM THE BEACH TO VOLCANIC ROCK

In the north the route travels from ⑫ *Péreybère* → p. 40 through ⑬ *Grand Baie* → p. 33 to ⑭ *Trou aux Biches* → p. 44 and past property owned by lots of rich Mauritians. The beaches, which are beautiful for bathing and snorkelling, are very busy indeed at weekends. Grand Baie, a lively small town, is the region's tourist centre. At ⑮ *Pointe aux Piments* → p. 42 the beaches become stony. The area is littered with lava debris, and the rocks that have been piled up by workers in the fields look like massive, ancient burial mounds. Beyond the fields stand the remains of volcanic craters. The road now leads away from the coast. It's worth making a detour to ⑯ *Triolet* → p. 44 to visit the largest Hindu temple on the island, and to ⑰ *Pamplemousses* → p. 38 where you should have at least a short stroll through the Botanical Garden (photo above left) before heading back to Port Louis.

230km/140mi. Driving time 4 hours.
Recommended travel time: one day.
A detailed map of the route can be found on the back cover, in the road atlas and the pull-out map

# THE NORTH

**,The North', which is how the region's referred to on motorway signs, begins where the suburbs of Port Louis end. Just one glance at the map will tell you that this region is flat and rather sparsely populated.**

Even towns such as Triolet, Goodlands and Pamplemousses consist of just one main street with some shops and a few houses in the side streets. The landscape is planted with sugar cane. Country roads, so straight they look as if they've been drawn with a ruler, shoot across the fields. If you're travelling here between March and September, you'll drive for miles and miles through a lush, green landscape. Just before the harvest, it may even feel as if you're driving between two green walls. At this time, the view extends only as far as the next bend

and the sky is seen in narrow, blue strips. Despite its extensive agriculture, the north is the most developed region for tourists. This is because the beaches and bays are picturesque, the sun shines over the sea throughout the afternoon, and there's isn't a more beautiful place in the world to watch it set in the evening. The reason for the development of tourism here is most likely the weather. In the north the island has particularly low levels of rainfall, meaning a lot of time has to be spent irrigating the sugar cane fields.

The region's tourist centre is the town of Grand Baie which lies on a turquoise bay. Yachts and fishing boats bob around in the natural harbour. There are lots of eateries and bars on the main street, and boutiques and souvenir shops are

---

Photo: The beach of Trou aux Biches

**A great destination for water sport fans, gourmets and night owls: no part of the island is more geared-up for tourists than the north**

clustered around small squares that can be found down various small streets. Several shopping centres have been built in recent years, including the Sunset Boulevard with its cafés and elegant shops.

# GRAND BAIE

(118 B–C 2–3) (*D E4*) **Grand Baie is regarded as the Côte d'Azur of Mauritius. This lively small town is a top destination for those seeking a wealth of experiences.**

Grand Baie is the centre of Mauritian cuisine, which can be sampled at the ● many food stalls on the streets and on the promenade. It's a colourful spectacle by the ● harbour when the fishermen come back with their catch, which they sell directly from the quay *(daily from around 1pm at the end of the car park)*. The town is also a centre for nightlife. In addition, because of the beautiful bay, it's also a hub for sailors and water sport lovers. Grand Baie's two colourful Hindu temples are also well worth a visit.

Great for those who don't want to dive: a stroll under the water

## FOOD & DRINK

### INSIDER TIP LE CAPITAINE
Enjoy the first class cuisine and excellent seafood with a view over the bay. *Daily | Royal Road | tel. 2 63 68 67 | Moderate–Expensive*

### DON CAMILLO
Popular, chic restaurant with snacks and Italian cuisine from antipasti to pizza. Daily | *Royal Road | tel. 2 63 85 40 | Budget*

### PALAIS DE CHINE
Among the island's many Chinese restaurants, the Palais de Chine is one of the best. Crab is their speciality. *Daily | Royal Road | tel. 2 63 71 20 | Moderate*

## SHOPPING

The small boutiques along the Royal Road are particularly aimed at a younger audience. They have an enormous selection of beach and leisurewear on offer.

### BAZAR DE GRAND BAIE
Tucked away in the narrow streets near the La Jonque Restaurant is this small market that sells fruit, vegetables, clothing and fashion accessories. *Daily 9am–5pm | Racket Road*

### GRAND BAIE CENTRE COMMERCIAL
Modern shops, an internet café, pharmacy and children's play area are all grouped together in a well-equipped supermarket. *Mon–Sat 9am–8.30pm, Sun 9am–1.30pm | La Salette Road*

### INSIDER TIP SUNSET BOULEVARD
This shopping arcade has a great ambience. Its selection of first class shops mainly sell clothing. *Mon–Sat 9.30am–6pm, irregular opening hours on Sundays | Royal Road*

## SPORTS & ACTIVITIES

### SWIMMING
The bay at Grand Baie is full of ships. You can only swim at the hotel's beaches and

from the popular small beach *La Cuvette* (118 B2) *(ю E4)* next to Le Royal Palm hotel. Wide, sandy beaches are located to the north and south of the city, along the road to *Péreybère* (118 C2) *(ю E3)*, at the *Pointe aux Canonniers* (118 B2) *(ю D3)* I *(10–15 minutes by bus)* and in the direction of *Trou aux Biches*. At the weekend these beaches are hubs for city dwellers who come to swim and picnic here and who ● make the beach their dance floor in the evenings.

## DEEP SEA FISHING
The company *Sportfisher (on the pier on Sunset Boulevard | tel. 2 63 83 58)* has several boats and teams that will help you with your fishing needs.

## HORSE RIDING DELIGHTS
You can explore the 750 hectares of lush vegetation in the Mont Choisy Leisure park on horseback. A visit to the Colonial House will take you on a trip back into the past. A horseback ride with refreshments costs 1800 rupees. Trips start at 8am or 4.30pm and last approx. 90 minutes. *Mont Choisy Sugar Estate | tel. 2 65 61 59*

## THE ISLANDS IN THE NORTH ★
A trip on the racing catamaran, the Harris Wilson, is a dream, and not just for sailors. Popular destinations include *Île Plate* (O)*(ю F1–2)* and *Îlot Gabriel* (O) *(ю O)*, which boast white beaches and snorkelling spots. A barbecue is served on board at midday. Price: approx. 2500 rupees including meals and drinks. *Croisières Australes | Coastal Road | tel. 2 63 16 69 | www.croisieres-australes.mu*

## DIVING
Several diving centres organise excursions to the diving locations in the north such as

*Pointe Vacoas, Aquarium* and *Flat Island*. *Mascareignes Plongée (Royal Road | tel. 2 69 12 65)* and diving schools at hotels.

## WATERSPORTS CENTRE ●
*Solarseawalk (Royal Road | tel. 2 63 78 19)* offers walks under water. With a helmet on your head that has a supply of air pumped in, you can stroll across the seabed and feed the fish at a depth of about three to four metres.

## ENTERTAINMENT

### BARS AND RESTAURANTS
Most of the bars in Grand Baie are well attended every night. A mainly younger crowd meets in the bars and discos, which stay open late into the night. The cocktail lists are usually longer than the food menus. Popular meeting spots in-

---

★ **Islands in the north**
Travel by sailing ship to the north's magnificent beaches and snorkelling spots → p. 35

★ **Botanical Garden**
Once a governor's vegetable garden, this is a heavenly piece of land, famous for its water lily and lotus ponds → p. 38

★ **Shivalah Temple**
The largest Hindu temple on Mauritius → p. 44

★ **Le Pescatore**
Considered one of the best restaurants on the island → p. 44

★ **Diving**
Hugue Vitry takes tourists off into shark territory → p. 45

**MARCO POLO HIGHLIGHTS**

clude the *Banana Café* and the Buddha Bar, where you can also go dancing. The *Cocoloko Bar* with its tropical garden and a large selection of their own cocktails is also popular.

This cult disco in the centre of the town is always well frequented, even in the low season. Partygoers of all nationalities come to the vaulted cellar where the

Time to relax: Le Royal Palm offers its guests an experience of pure luxury

### BEACH HOUSE ●
A meeting place for locals and international visitors alike. Whether you're wearing flip-flops or a suit, everyone's welcome at the bar. It's this diversity that gives it its charm. Located just a few steps from the shore, it has a view looking out over the wide bay. *Tue–Sun from 11.30am | Royal Road | tel. 2 63 25 99 | www.thebeachhouse.mu*

### LES ENFANTS TERRIBLES
A bar and nightclub with a medium-sized dance floor and a large terrace that attracts a rather affluent clientele. They play a colourful mix of tunes with a slight preference for 80s' music. *Wed, Fri, Sat from 10.30pm | Royal Road | Pointe aux Canonniers*

high life reigns until the small hours of the morning. The playlist includes techno, dance, disco and sometimes reggae. *Daily from 10pm | Royal Road | next to the filling station.*

## WHERE TO STAY

### LE CANONNIER
Situated between Trou aux Biches and Grand Baie on a peninsula, this hotel is ideal for families with children. The kids' club is located in an old lighthouse. The complex nestles in a tropical garden surrounded by the beautiful, azure-blue sea. Three small beaches, a large pool and a wide range of sports are on offer. *284 rooms | Royal Road | Pointe aux Canonniers | tel. 2 09 70 00 | www.beachcomber-hotels.com | Expensive*

## ESPRIT LIBRE

André and Stéphane run this small, friendly guesthouse with an adjoining restaurant on the cape of Pointe aux Canonniers. *5 bedrooms, 2 apartments | Rue Bourdet | tel. 2 69 11 59 | www.esprit libremaurice.com | Budget*

## GRAND BAY SUITES

A self-catering apartment complex in the centre of Grand Baie. 25 apartments with living room/bedroom, modern kitchen and terrace or balcony. The supermarket is right next door, and restaurants and shops are just a few minutes' walk away. *Royal Road | tel. 2 65 52 61 | www.grand baysuites.com | Budget–Moderate*

## GRAND BAY TRAVEL TOURS

A good selection of well-kept, self-catering bungalows and apartments within walking distance of the beach. *tel. 2 65 52 61 | www.gbtt.com | Budget–Moderate*

## MERVILLE BEACH

Ideal for people who want a laid-back beach holiday, this hotel lies on a beautiful sandy beach in the north, not far from Grand Baie. Rooms are located in the main house or in small cottages. *169 rooms | Royal Road | tel. 2 09 22 00 | www.naiade.com | Expensive*

## OCEAN VILLAS

A small complex with self-catering rooms, apartments and bungalows on a beach in Grand Baie. Suitable for holidaymakers (and especially families) on a limited budget. It's in a quiet location, but is nevertheless not far from supermarkets, restaurants, bars and nightclubs. *25 bungalows, 6 rooms | Royal Road | tel. 2 63 67 88 | www.ocean-villas. com | Budget*

## LE ROYAL PALM

Pure elegance, and luxurious down to the last detail, this hotel is the most exlcusive on the island and is situated on a white, sandy beach, with a beautiful clifftop bar and a new beauty and massage salon. Rooms start from 24,000 rupees. *57 rooms, 27 suites | Royal Road | tel. 2 09 83 00 | www.beachcomber-hotels. com | Expensive*

## VERANDA HOTEL

This hotel offers guests an intimate atmosphere. It's located right next to the

# LOW BUDGET

▶ Saturday brunch in *Café Müller*: from September to June between 10am and 2pm you can have an excellent continental brunch in this café for 400 rupees (reservation recommended). As the name suggests, it's a German-run café, and it has a lovely grassy garden. *Royal Road | Grand Baie | tel. 2 63 52 30 | www.cafe-mul ler.restaurant.mu*

▶ Excursion tips: trips on public buses only cost a couple of rupees. Because the buses mainly operate over long distances, you can also use them to take an individual sightseeing tour. Tell the driver your destination and have your change ready. The buses are often full in the mornings and evenings. There aren't any timetables, and with a little bit of luck the buses will stop for you in remote villages, even where there's no official stop, if you wave them down. Ask about the different routes at your hotel's reception desk.

Yacht Club, around 15 minutes' walk from the town centre. There's also a diving centre (PADI courses, tel. 2 63 80 16). *62 rooms | Royal Road | tel. 2 66 97 00 | www.veranda-resorts.com | Moderate*

INFORMATION

## INFORMATION

### GRAND BAY TRAVEL

This organisation provides tours of the island and information about possible excursions. You can even book helicopter tours. *Mon–Fri 9am–6pm | Royal Road | In the town centre | tel. 2 63 87 71*

## WHERE TO GO

### GOODLANDS (119 D3) *(∅ F4)*

Goodlands is a typical, small Mauritian town situated 9km/5mi east of Grand Baie. The town consists of a crowded main street and various small side streets that branch off into residential areas. The shops' goods spill out onto the pavements. A busy ● fruit and vegetable market is held here on Wednesday and Saturday mornings. It's situated on the town's eastern outskirts and textiles are sold on Thursdays and Fridays.

Hardly any tourists come here, and those that do usually come to visit the factory located across from the Historic Marine market. This workshop has been producing model ships of the highest quality since 1982. You can watch the craftsmen at work with their materials *(Mon–Fri 9am–5pm)*. The showroom's also open on Saturdays *(Sat 9am–noon | Historic Marine | Free entry)*.

A *kayak tour* heads for *Île d'Ambre*, through Mangrove forests, and carries on between small islands out to the sea. You'll set up camp on one of the islands. The next morning you'll take a snorkelling break before paddling through the fishing village of *Grand Gaube* and on to

*Calodyne*. Excursions start from Goodlands from where you'll take a minibus to St Antoine. The tour costs from 2500 rupees. *Tel. 7 52 00 46 | www.yemayaadventures.com*

# PAMPLE-MOUSSES

(118 B5) *(∅ E5)* **This small provincial town lies half an hour's drive to the northeast of Port Louis. Its historical significance is evident thanks to the presence of oldest church on the island, which has made the town its home.**

Today, the town plays host both to small industries and the largest public hospital on the island. The urban landscape does not inspire any great enthusiasm. The main streets only offer the usual chains of shops, bars and fast food outlets. Were it not for the Botanical Gardens, Pamplemousses would hardly be worth a mention.

## SIGHTSEEING

### THE BOTANICAL GARDEN ★ ●

Back in 1735, it's pretty certain that Governor Mahé de Labourdonnais would never have dreamed that his vegetable garden would one day become a Royal Botanical Garden and Mauritius's principal place of interest. His advisor, businessman Pierre Poivre, however, had great things in mind from the beginning when he took over supervision of the site in 1770: he wanted to make Mauritius a spice island, break the Dutch monopoly and deliver the goods from his garden to the whole world. He also cultivated orchids and ornamental plants in order to export them.

Today the park's used for recreation and education. Although it's only a few hundred hectares in size, it hardly lacks a single plant that flourishes in this tropical climate. Hiring one of the many guides is recommended because they can tell you interesting facts about the plants and their uses. (A one-hour tour costs 75 rupees per person.) In addition, there's also an enclosure with giant tortoises, an old sugar mill, the castle *Mon Plaisir*, a colonial villa dating from 1777, and a wrought iron entrance gate that was displayed and won first prize at the Great Exhibition at Crystal Palace in London in 1851. At the weekend many locals come here to have a picnic. *Daily 8.30am–5.30pm | Entry 100 rupees*

### THE CHURCH OF ST FRANÇOIS D'ASSISE

This church with its simple façade and impressive wooden beams in the nave was the first church built on the island (1756). In fact, it was even here before the town itself. The ● cemetery is also definitely worth a look. The vicarage dating from 1737 is thought to be the oldest building on Mauritius.

### INSIDER TIP L'AVENTURE DU SUCRE

Diagrams, exhibits and interactive displays give information about the history and processing of cane sugar, the island's agriculture, and the 'waste product' of sugar, rum. The restaurant can also be recommended. *Beau Plan | 300m from the Botanical Garden | Mon–Sun 9am–5pm | Entry 350 rupees | www.aventure dusucre.com*

## FOOD & DRINK

### INSIDER TIP CAFÉ WIENER WALZER (VALSE DE VIENNE)

In the 'Viennese Waltz Garden Café' you can enjoy a quiet location and nice atmosphere, for once not having to sit by the road, and there's also delicious Black Forest gateau. Snacks are also available.

Look and be amazed: the Botanical Garden's glorious tropical plants and flowers

*Daily | Powder Mill Road | behind the church | tel. 2 43 05 60 | Budget–Moderate*

### LE PLAISIR DE POIVRE

A restaurant located opposite the Botanical Garden with a dining room that opens onto the street. Creole and European cuisine. Only open for lunch. *Daily | Royal Road | tel. 2 43 85 29 | Budget-Moderate*

## SHOPPING

### MARITIME MODELS CO. LTD.
You can see sailing boat models being made in this factory *(Royal Road, behind the Botanical Garden)*. You can also visit the factory's shop situated in the Pamplemousses Commercial Centre *(tel. 2 43 93 47)*.

## WHERE TO GO

### CHÂTEAU DE LABOURDONNAIS
(118 C4) (*ØJ E5*)
This château is located in the middle of a park in the small town of Mapou. The building, constructed in 1859 and still family-owned, is now open to the public after the completion of extensive renovation work. Walking through the rooms you'll feel yourself transported back into the 19th century. After visiting the villa you're invited to stroll through the garden with its magnificent arboretum, which includes 100 year-old mango, nutmeg and clove trees. On the site there's also a rum distillery, a bar where you can try the liquor made from sugar cane, and a restaurant that offers menus from the colonial times. *Daily 9am–5pm | tel. 2 66 95 33 | www.unchateaudanslanature. com | Budget–Moderate*

# PÉREYBÈRE & CAP MAL-HEUREUX

(118 C2) (*ØJ E3*) **The small seaside resort of Péreybère lies just a short distance north of Grand Baie and is situated on a bay with a beautiful beach.**
Colourful beach towels and other souvenirs flutter in the wind, and nearby small restaurants offer tables in the shade of the filao trees. The town is quieter than Grand Baie, and a pair of small, simple hotels and many apartments offer rooms that are very popular with families, backpackers and young people.
Just a short way further on lies *Cap Malheureux*, the 'Cape of Bad Luck'. In clear

The fishermen at Cap Malheureux work hard in the most beautiful weather

weather you can see out over the small islands of Coin de Mire, *Île Plate* and *Île Ronde* with their steep cliffs. The coast is rugged and barren here. It's unclear whether the cape gained its name because of the many ships that ran aground here, or due to the nearby French defeat by the English, who then advanced on Port Louis. Private villas along the coast block the sea view. You can only enjoy the panoramic view right on the cape next to the wooden church, the *Église de Cap Malheureux*, which stands out thanks to its red roof.

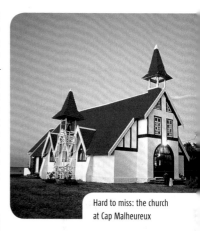
Hard to miss: the church at Cap Malheureux

## FOOD & DRINK

### LE COIN DE MIRE
This small restaurant lies diagonally opposite the church of Cap Malheureux and offers good, local cooking. In the same building, there are 14 apartments that can be rented cheaply. *Daily | tel. 262 8070 | Budget*

### JULIE'S CLUB
Popular bar in Péreybère wth a good selection of cocktails. They occasionally have karaoke evenings. *Daily | Royal Road | tel. 778 8483 | www.juliesclub-mauritius.com | Budget–Moderate*

### PALM BEACH CAFÉ
Located right on the magnificent beach at Péreybère. They sell light bites such as salads, crêpes and sandwiches, and also fresh fish from the grill. Family-run and popular with the locals. *Daily | Plage Publique | Péreybère | tel. 263 5821 | Budget–Moderate*

### RESTAURANT AMIGO
Despite the restaurant's 50 tables, you can enjoy lobster and seafood in a peaceful atmosphere. There are also Mauritian cari dishes on offer. The wall serves as a rather unusual guestbook. Reservations are recommended and there's a free shuttle service for holidaymakers in the area. *Mon–Sat | Le Pavillon | Cap Malheureux | tel. 262 8418 | Moderate–Expensive*

## SPORTS & ACTIVITIES

INSIDER TIP ► **SAILING TOURS ON A CATAMARAN**
This experienced crew offers sailing tours with a chance to stay the night on board. The trip also includes a diving course and a visit of the offshore islands of *Coin de Mire* (118 C1) (*Ω E2–3*), *Île Plate, Îlot Gabriel* (0) (*Ω F2*) and a few coastal towns. Tailor-made programmes are combined with good service and comfort. The minimum duration is two days. *Information and prices at Magic Sails Mauritius | tel. 262 7188 | www.magicsails.mu*

## WHERE TO STAY

### CÔTE D'AZUR
A small hotel in the centre of Péreybère opposite the public beach. *18 rooms | Royal Road | tel. 263 8165 | Budget*

## KUXVILLE BEACH COTTAGES AND SERENDIP ☆

The history of Kuxville goes back half a century to when Helmut Otto Wilhelm Kux decided to settle here. From his small beach house, he developed a family-run bungalow resort complete with its own diving and kitesurfing schools, which lies in a sheltered bay with a view lonial times and create a unique atmosphere. Whether catamaran trips, underwater walks or deep-sea fishing is your thing, tourists are offered a wide, generally free programme of activities. Good cuisine and a peaceful location. *64 rooms | Anse La Raie | Cap Malheureux | tel. 2 04 40 00 | www.paradisecovehotel. com | Expensive*

A hotel for romantics: the Paradise Cove Hotel located on a turquoise-blue lagoon

of the offshore islands of Mauritius. Servants are on hand to cook evening meals for guests on request. The resort provides ideal accommodation for families. *21 bungalows | on Cap Malheureux | tel. 2 62 88 36 | www.kuxville.com | Budget–Moderate*

### INSIDER TIP ▶ PARADISE COVE HOTEL

The rooms and suites of the island's most romantic hotel are situated around a man-made lagoon. The lovingly created facilities have Indian influences from co-

# POINTE AUX PIMENTS

**(118 A4) (⑰ D4) Several luxury hotels stretch along the fine sandy beaches from here right down to the Bay of Balaclava.**

There are wonderful spots for snorkelling in front of the bay, at the mouth of the *Rivière Citron* in the *Baie aux Tortues (Turtle Bay)*. The coral reef is easily reachable and is not far from the beach. Aside from the hotels, there's hardly any infrastructure at all.

## FOOD & DRINK

### SOLEIL COUCHANT

Simple, but good. The menu includes curry dishes and delicacies. You can also rent simple rooms here. *Daily | Royal Road | tel. 2 61 67 86 | Budget*

## SPORTS & ACTIVITIES

### MAURITIUS AQUARIUM

This small aquarium provides insight into the underwater world of Mauritius without getting your feet wet. Families with children should try to get to the INSIDER TIP fish feeding around 11am. *Mon–Sat 9.30am–5pm, Sun 10am–3pm | Entry 250 rupees | Coastal Road | tel. 2 61 45 61 | www.mauritiusaquarium.com |*

### INSIDER TIP YEMAYA ADVENTURES

Patrick Haberland offers hikes and much more besides. Participants' efforts are rewarded when they get to see the wonderful natural beauty of Mauritius. From ⚡ *Le Pouce* you'll get a wonderful view of the north of the island. *www.yemaya adventures.com*

## WHERE TO STAY

### MARITIME HOTEL

This spacious complex at Turtle Bay, a protected natural park, offers a nine-hole golf course (par 29) and riding stables. The clientele, mainly British and German, come from the higher echelons of society. A cosy bar nestles between the pool and the sea, and one of the three restaurants is integrated into the ruins of Balaclava. *218 rooms | Balaclava | Turtle Bay | tel. 2 40 10 00 | www.maritim.de | Expensive*

### THE OBEROI ⚡

In the grounds of this luxury hotel there are elegant villas with private swimming pools, nestling in a garden. It offers a stunning view of the sea. Privacy, exclusivity and perfect service are all included. *76 rooms | Turtle Bay | tel. 2 04 36 00 | www.oberoihotels.com | Expensive*

### LE RÉCIF

A cheerfully furnished, modern complex with a small spa, visited primarily by families and young couples. They offer sports facilities, including diving and boating tours. *70 rooms | Royal Road | tel. 2 61 04 44 | www.lerecif.com | Expensive*

### LE VICTORIA

A modern resort with a lively atmosphere on a wide beach. The complex includes a large pool, good restaurants, several bars, evening entertainment and many sports facilities. The recreational facilities for children and teens make this a popular resort for families. *246 rooms | Pointe aux Piments | tel. 2 04 20 00 | www.beachcomber-hotels.com | Moderate–Expensive*

### VILLAS MON PLAISIR

This renovated, family-run resort with a diving centre attached is a good starting point for the more adventurous. *41 rooms | Royal Road | tel. 2 61 66 00 | www.villasmonplaisir.com | Budget–Moderate*

## WHERE TO GO

### LA NICOLIÈRE RESERVOIR

(118 C6) (𝕞 E6)
The La Nicolière reservoir is located in the interior of the island near Villebague. You'll get a magnificent view of the east and west coasts from the ⚡ INSIDER TIP road that leads along the lake to Nouvelle Découverte. Perhaps you'll even see

A home for Shiva, Brahma and Vishnu: the Shivalah Hindu temple complex in Triolet

monkeys climbing in the dense foliage of the *Nicolière Mountains.*

### SHIVALAH TEMPLE ★
(118 B3) (*🗺 D4*)
The largest Hindu temple complex in Mauritius is located at the northern end of Triolet. The construction of the *Maheswarnath Temple*, the main building of the complex, was begun in 1891. It's richly adorned with colourfully painted deities. *Shivalah Road*

# TROU AUX BICHES

(118 B3) (*🗺 D4*) **When people talk about Trou aux Biches, they're thinking less about the small village itself and more of its beautiful beach.**
Especially at weekends it's the destination for thousands of sightseers, particularly Indian families. The gleaming white beach may once have seemed glamorous but, compared with the other more modern facilities, the ambience is now disappointing.

## FOOD & DRINK

### LA CRAVACHE D'OR
Freshly caught fish and delicious meat dishes are served here right by the shore. An elegant setting and a good wine menu. *Daily | Royal Road | tel. 2 65 70 21 | Expensive*

### LE PESCATORE ★
Guests sit on a veranda in an elegant atmosphere right by the pier and enjoy the view of the sea. Locals recommend Le Pescatore as the best gourmet restaurant on the island. *Daily | Route Cotière | tel. 2 65 63 37 (Reservation required) | Expensive*

### DIVING ⭐

Hugue Vitry from the *Blue Water Diving Center* offers tours to old shipwrecks and to the INSIDER TIP *Whale Rock sea cliffs*. He also offers adventurous night diving trips and visits to the *Shark's Pit* where up to 40 sharks swim all around you. A dive costs about 16,000 rupees including equipment. *Royal Road | tel. 2657186 | www. bluewaterdivingcenter.com*

### SUBMARINE TOURS

The Blue Safari submarine dives down to the coral reefs to a depth of up to 40m. With a sub scooter, an underwater vehicle that you control yourself, you can go for trips in the shallow waters down to a maximum of approx. 3m. *Submarine approx. 3900, scooter 5000 rupees | Blue Safari Submarine | Trou aux Biches (near the Hotel Coralia Mont Choisy) | tel. 263 3333 | www.blue-safari.com*

### BIRD'S NEST

A small family holiday resort for self-caterers. The bungalows can accommodate five to seven people. The resort features a large pool, and two villas even have their own. Beautiful location on the sea between Trou aux Biches and Mont Choisy. *8 Holiday Apartments, 2 Villas | Coastal Road | tel. 2655341 | Budget*

### LE CARDINAL

A small, exclusive resort with 13 luxurious suites on a long white sandy beach at Trou aux Biches. The design is elegant and cool, something the penthouse shows off to its fullest advantage. *tel. 2045200 | www.lecardinalresort.com | Expensive*

### CASUARINA HOTEL

A charming resort in the style of a Mediterranen village. The rooms and apartments surround two pools and are separated from the beach by the coastal road. *93 rooms | 15 bungalows | Coastal Road | tel. 2045000 | casuarina@intnet.mu | Moderate*

### LE GRAND BLEU

Simple rooms and apartments, 50m from the beach. There's a small restaurant, a bar with a pool table and a diving school nearby. *63 rooms | Royal Road | tel. 2655812 | Budget*

### TROU AUX BICHES RESORT & SPA HOTEL

This resort lies on one of the island's most beautiful beaches and is surrounded by a tropical garden. All villas and beachfront and senior beachfront suites come with their own pools. There are also several pools available for guests staying in other suites. Six restaurants provide a great amount of culinary variety. *316 suites and 16 villas | tel. 2046565 | www.beachcomber-hotels.com | Expensive*

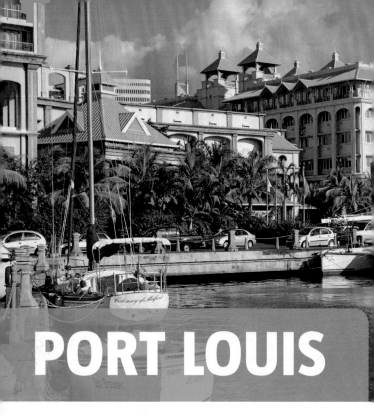

# PORT LOUIS

▨▨▨ **MAP INSIDE BACK COVER**
**Port Louis (121 D–E 1–2) (∭ D6)**, the capital city, is the island's hub. The government meets here and it boasts not only the main harbour and long beaches, but also museums, churches, pagodas, temples and mosques.

However, Port Louis (170,000 inhabitants) seems like a bustling small town, an impression that not even the modern, high-rise office blocks can change. The silhouettes of these buildings have to compete with the 823m/2700ft-high mountain range that goes half way round the city and defines its limits. The city isn't very large and a round tour won't take more than one or two hours. Port Louis was founded in 1736 by the French Governor Mahé de Labourdon-

> **CITY** **WHERE TO START?**
> **The Statue of Mahé de Labourdonnais (U B2–3) (∭ b2–3):** If you've come by car, park at the Caudan Waterfront Complex (a fee is charged) and go through the subway to the statue at the market in the centre of the Old Town. Taxis can also drop you off here. Bus passengers come either from the Main North Bus Station or the Regional South Bus Station.

nais. He created a rectangular network of streets, expanded the harbour and erected Government House and the island's defensive fortifications. Since then,

Photo: Port Louis harbour and the Caudan Waterfront Complex

This is where the heart of the island beats: the bustling capital city is characterised by the coexistence of peoples, religions and cultures

the city has often been destroyed by fires and natural catastrophes, most recently at the end of the 19th century due to a particularly violent cyclone. What remains of the colonial architecture, however, is frequently in need of renovation today. Only a small historic district near Government House has been restored. The city is loud. Thousands of cars crawl through the streets, mopeds rattle by, and people of all colours throng the pavements on which traders spread out their wares. Port Louis is a hot, busy cauldron of activity during the day. Around 6pm, however, all of the shops close and everyone disappears. Suddenly you'll think you're in a ghost town.

## SIGHTSEEING

### AAPRAVASI GHAT ● (U C1–2) (*🗺 c1–2*)

After the British abolished slavery in Mauritius in 1834, the state required new workers. These were hired from the northern provinces and from the south and southeast of India. These labourers committed themselves to working in Mauritius for several years. In return, their passage on ships was paid for and they received room and board in addition to a small sal-

## BLUE PENNY MUSEUM ●
(U A2–3) (𝄞 a2–3)

This museum's exhibition revolves around the island's art and history. There's a

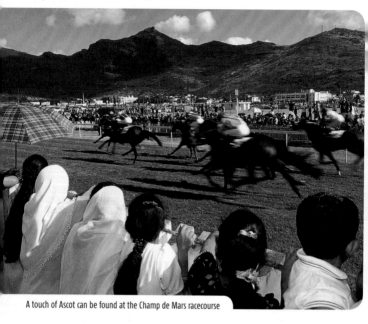

A touch of Ascot can be found at the Champ de Mars racecourse

ary. A transit camp was built in the harbour in 1849, which constantly had to be expanded due to the large increase in immigration. The camp remained open until 1923. During this time, this camp was the point of arrival for some 450,000 contracted workers, a flow of immigrants that ranks among one of the largest migrations in history. Although few of the buildings are preserved today, the complex was declared a Unesco World Heritage Site in 2006. Guided tours give you an impression of the economic and social conditions in the 19th century. Aapravasi Ghat is located to the north of the post office in the harbour. It's free to visit. *Mon–Sat 9am–4pm | www.aapravasighat.org*

navigation room devoted to models of ships, old maps and nautical instruments. The museum's greatest treasure is the original, unused version of the legendary postage stamp, the ★ 'Blue Mauritius'. *Caudan Waterfront | Mon–Sat 10am–4.30pm | Entry 225 rupees*

## CHAMP DE MARS ★ ●
(U E–F 5–6) (𝄞 e–f 5–6)

The Champ de Mars racecourse is home to the Mauritius Turf Club which holds horse races here every Saturday from May to November. Founded in 1812, it is, after Ascot, the second oldest in the world. Up to 40,000 visitors gather here on race days, creating an unrivalled funfair atmosphere. Main entrance in D'Estaing Street | Dates and prices: www.mauritiusturfclub.com

## CHINATOWN (U C–D 1–2) (𝄐 c–d 1–2)

Many of the houses here date from the period around 1900. Although most are in need of such extensive renovation that they will now be almost impossible to save, they convey an idea of what a splendid city this must once have been. Small shops and arts and craft businesses are located on the ground floor, and people live on the floors above. The small shops that sell household goods, hardware and Chinese deities and medicines are mainly geared towards the locals, but they're also interesting for visitors, and seem much more exotic than the tourist shops. There are a few good Chinese restaurants here and there's always a wonderful aroma of spicy dishes in the air. The narrow streets are always full and there's a permanent hustle and bustle even after closing time and at weekends.

## FORT ADELAIDE ● ☆
### (U E–F 3–4) (𝄐 e–f 3–4)

This fort was built in 1834 on top of the 100m/330ft-high Petite Montaigne. Its architects were the English, who at that time were fearful of French attempts to recapture the island. The view over the city from here is excellent. The inner courtyard of the fort is also sometimes used as an open-air stage. Sebastopol Street | Information: www.tourism-mauritius.mu under 'Events Calendar' and on www.otayo.com

## INSIDER TIP ▶ PHOTOGRAPHY MUSEUM
### (U C4) (𝄐 c4)

Formed from a private collection, the museum is like a treasure chest full of old cameras, photos and scenery used in earlier workshops. At the end of Rue du Vieux Conseil pedestrian zone, opposite the theatre | Mon–Fri 9.30am–3pm | Entry 150 rupees

---

**MARCO POLO HIGHLIGHTS**

### ★ 'Blue Mauritius'
Particularly valuable because it's not been franked: the world's most famous postage stamp is shown in the Blue Penny Museum → p. 48

### ★ Champ de Mars
Parades and horse races on the Champ de Mars: from May to November a real carnival atmosphere reigns at the racetrack. → p. 48

### ★ Natural History Museum
Learn about the island's fauna, flora and geology – and even about long-extinct animals → p. 50

### ★ Central Market
A colourful hustle and bustle around stalls with exotic goods. If they don't have it, it doesn't exist. → p. 52

### ★ Caudan Waterfront
A modern shopping complex with a casino → p. 54

### ★ Eureka
A prime example of Creole architecture that's been turned into a museum → p. 57

### ★ Kalaisson Temple
Discover the colourful world of the Hindu gods in this temple complex → p. 57

## CHURCHES

With its unembellished grey walls and two chunky towers, the Catholic St Louis Cathedral (Church Street, on the Cathedral Square) (U D4) (*m d4*), seems like a fortress. It's also rather plain inside. In front of the cathedral is a fountain, built in 1786, which for a long time provided the population of the upper part of the city with water from Le Pouce Mountain. Behind the church is the 18th century bishop's residence that looks captivating with its large veranda and beautiful gardens. The Anglican *St James Cathedral* on Poudrière Street (U D5) (*m d5*) is more modestly decorated.

## INSIDER TIP MOSQUES

There are two large mosques in the town centre. Although the high minaret of the mosque on the corner of Ramgoolam Street and Eugène Laurent Street (U D3) (*m d3*) is eye catching, it otherwise offers nothing much worth seeing. In contrast, the other mosque is like a small fairy-tale palace with its playful oriental architecture: the *Jummah Mosque (Jummah Mosque Street/Royal Street | Sat–Wed 9.30am–noon, only outside prayer times)* (U C–D2) (*m c–d2*) was built between 1850 and 1885. Filigree decorations adorn the rooms and the inner courtyard and the courtyard is home to an almond tree, which is said to have been here before the building itself. Women and non-Muslim visitors may only visit the atrium, from which you can, however, get a glimpse of the prayer hall. Men are expected to have covered arms and legs.

## NATURAL HISTORY MUSEUM ★ ● (U B3) (*m b3*)

This museum's comprehensive resources explain the island's flora, fauna and geology. Although it's set out rather quaintly, you'll be particularly impressed by the department of Marine Life. The museum's most spectacular exhibits are the INSIDER TIP skeleton of a solitaire, a flightless bird that lived on the island of Rodrigues, and the reconstruction of a dodo complete with feathers. The library, housed on the first floor, is considered the best archive about the islands of the Indian Ocean. *Chaussee Street | Mon/Tue/Thu/Fri 9am–4pm, Sat/Sun 9am–noon | Free entry*

## PAGODAS

There are three large pagodas in the south of Port Louis where most of the Chinese people live. The largest is the Lam Soon Tin *How Pagoda* (U F5) (*m f5*), right on the southeastern side of the Champ de Mars on Eugène Laurent Street. It's a gloomy building, but also houses an impressive altar with large statues. The *Lim Fad Temple* (0) (*m 0*) (on *Volcy Pougnet Street*, also called Rue

Madame), with its high gate and rich colours, injects a touch of Beijing into an otherwise rather pale area. Only two streets further on, in *Justice Street*, stands the *Thien Thane Pagoda* (O) *(𝄞 O)*. This tower, with its three arched roofs, rises gracefully up against the backdrop of the steep sides of the mountains beyond. The place buzzes with activity on Chinese holidays, but is otherwise quiet.

### POSTAL MUSEUM (U B2) *(𝄞 b2)*

The Museum's exhibits include postage stamps from around the world, and telegraph equipment and other apparatus. *In the Post Office at the harbour | Mon–Fri 9.30am–4.30pm, Sat 10am–4pm | Entry 150 rupees*

### GOVERNMENT HOUSE (U C3) *(𝄞 c3)*

The French governors truly spared no expense when they extended and added new floors to this building between 1729 and 1807. No other building on the island characterises the French era quite so well. It seems all the more ironic, then, that sculptures of the governor Sir William Stevenson and the British Queen Victoria stand in the building's courtyard. The two figures look out on the statue of Mahé de Labourdonnais, who has to be content to stand 200m away over the fence. The buildings lie at the end of two avenues, Duke of Edinburgh Avenue and Queen Elizabeth Avenue. It's hardly used any more and is closed to visitors.

### CITY THEATRE (U C3–4) *(𝄞 c3–4)*

This building with its lovely façade, built between 1820 and 1822, is thought to be the first theatre in the southern hemisphere. Famous actors and musicians trod the boards here in the 19th century. Regular performances and events are being held here once again since its renova-

You can see a statue of Queen Elizabeth outside Government House

tion in 1995. In combination with the museum and the gallery in the pedestrian zone opposite, a veritable small pork. In the fourth market hall, souvenirs are on offer as well as textiles, leatherwork and arts and crafts.

Market women at the Marché Central waiting for customers

cultural centre has been created. *Gillet Square | behind Government House | Visits outside of show times are free*

### CENTRAL MARKET ★ (U C2) (*M c2*)

The cultural diversity of Mauritius is shown off to even greater advantage at the *Marché Central (Central Market)*, where there's a bewilderingly large variety of exotic wares on offer. Three of the four halls exclusively sell food. Some of these foodstuffs are lovingly displayed and arranged, but others are strewn across the tables and the floor with alarming carelessness. Bloody sheep heads lie next to coloured coral fish in the fish and meat section. Out of respect for Muslims, you have to go through a door to get to the separate section for

The market halls were built around 1840. They have, however, been destroyed by fires on several occasions, most recently in 1981. Despite this, the restored façades, the cobblestone alleyways and the ornate wrought-iron gates form a nostalgic image. Up to 40,000 people visit the market every day. *Opposite the Post Office between the motorway and Queen Street | Mon–Sat 6am–6pm, Sun 6am–noon, most stalls only open at 8 am, however*

## FOOD & DRINK

### LE CAFÉ DU VIEUX CONSEIL
### (U C4) (*M c4*)

A small oasis to stop and have a break, where you can buy salad, crêpes and sample a Creole menu. *Mon–Fri 11am–3pm | Rue du Vieux Conseil | tel. 2 11 03 93 | Moderate*

### CAUDAN WATERFRONT (U A2) (ⓜ a2)

Many fast food outlets, pubs and some speciality restaurants are located next to boutiques and jewellers in the shopping centre at the harbour. The Food Court with its Indian, Chinese and Creole selection is clustered around a sun terrace. It closes, just like the shops, at 5.30pm. The restaurants and bars, however, are open right through until the early hours of the morning.

At weekends ● bands play on the waterfront in the open air. Between 7pm and 9pm groups come out and showcase music in different styles. You can listen to jazz on Saturdays between noon and 2pm ands large crowds of people usually gather round the musicians quite quickly.

### INSIDER TIP ▶ INDRA RESTAURANT
(121 D2) (ⓜ D6)

This restaurant, complete with sitting cushions arranged across the floor and a fountain, is infused with a hint of the Arabian nights. The menu includes culinary delicacies from India. *Daily | Reservation recommended | Domaine les Pailles | tel. 2 86 42 25 | Expensive*

### LAMBIC RESTAURANT (U B4) (ⓜ b4)

This restaurant offers Mauritian and European cuisine and above all has a surprisingly large selection of international beers. *Mon–Sat | St. Georges Street | tel. 2 12 60 11 | Budget at noon, otherwise Expensive*

### SHEZAN (U D4) (ⓜ d4)

Pakistani cuisine is served here at lunchtime behind the St Louis cathedral. The food is something a little different and also affordable. *Mon–Fri | Corner of Gonnin/Geoffroy Street | tel. 2 10 25 25 | Budget*

### TANDOORI EXPRESS (U B2) (ⓜ b2)

This fast food restaurant in the Astrolabe building on the waterfront offers Indian food in no time at all in a bustling environment. Open at lunchtimes and in the evenings and has affordable menus. *Mon–Sat | Port Louis Waterfront | tel. 2 10 98 98 | Budget*

## LOW BUDGET

▶ Concerts by renowned Mauritian and some international artists are affordable on the island. Free performances are also organised for Mauritians now and then, at the Citadel in Port Louis, for example *(Mon–Sat, 9.30am–5.30pm)*. The current program of events and the ticket offices can be found at *www.otayo.com*.

▶ Around midday, street vendors sell snacks to the Mauritians working in Port Louis (roti, gâteaux piments, stuffed breads, soups). An especially good selection is available near the market, round the bus stations, and in front of the Natural History Museum.

▶ On *Corderie Street* **(U C2–3)** *(ⓜ c2–3)*, which begins at the harbour, there's one fabric shop after another. Here you will find cotton, linen, silk and rich fabrics artfully embroidered with pearls and sequins at fantastic prices. The sellers like to spread out their wares in front of you. *Mon–Fri, 9.30am–5pm*

## SHOPPING

### SHOPPING CENTRES

In both of the shopping centres at the harbour, ★ *Caudan Waterfront* (U A2) *(⚇ a2)* and *Port Louis Waterfront* (U B2) *(⚇ b2)*, there are numerous shops in a playful architectural style that's somewhere between colonial and post-modern. The many attractions include a casino, several cinemas and a hotel, as

years they've not only prepared tea blends to combat gastritis and asthma, cellulitis and haemorrhoids, but have also conjured up aphrodisiacs from their stacks of rustling leaves and dried fruits. The shop owners are proud to show off orders they've received from around the world, as well as letters from their newly cured clients. The stalls are located at the main entrance of the fruit and vegetable market hall.

Imaginatively designed – the Caudan Waterfront shopping centre

well as restaurants, bars and cafés. All of the leading fashion and leisurewear designers on the island have their own boutiques here. *Mon–Fri 9.30am–5.30pm, Sat 9.30am–7pm, Sun 9.30am–noon*

### INSIDER TIP ▶ HEALTH TEAS

There isn't an ailment in existence that doesn't have a herb growing to counteract it: at least that's the motto of the two herbalists on the central market (U C2) *(⚇ c2)*. For nearly the last 50

### JEWELLERY

Famous brand watches and diamond and gold jewellery are offered at low prices at *Poncini*. In order to buy duty free items, you must present your passport and your plane ticket and pay either in western currency or with a credit card. After purchase, the merchandise will then be handed to you before you leave the airport. *Mon–Fri 8.30am–4.15pm, Sat 8.30am–noon | Two branches: Jules Koenig Street opposite the City Theatre*

(U C4) *(map c4) and in the Caudan Water-front* (U A2) *(map a2)*

## ENTERTAINMENT

Almost everywhere in Port Louis seems to die out after closing time. However, there is an exception: the harbour's *Caudan Waterfront Shopping Complex* which was opened in 1997. This labyrinthine complex with its fanciful turrets, bay windows and pavilions is a magnificent, delicate pink delight that was frequented until recently by locals rather than by tourists. The generous grounds, with their courts, arcades and a promenade, feature bars, restaurants, cafés and cinemas. The Caudan Waterfront Complex is also a wonderful place for simply strolling around.

### CASINO (U A2) *(map a2)*

Visitors enter the casino in the Caudan Waterfront Complex through the bow of a lavishly designed pirate ship. They've also expended a lot of effort in the interior to keep the pirate theme going throughout. The ground floor *(open daily 10am–4am)* is full of rows of one-armed bandits. Up on the first floor *(daily 8pm–4am)*, you can try your luck at roulette, blackjack and poker.

### CINEMAS

In the centre of Port Louis there's still an old movie theatre that primarily plays Indian movies to a local audience. It's called the Cine *City Majestic* and is located on Poudrière Street (U D5) *(map d5)*. It's worth visiting as a curiosity for tourists *(Entry 150 rupees)*. The screen is massive, which lets the melodrama of Bollywood soar to even greater emotional heights. Apart from that, however, the building's facilities are unfortunately not very up to date.

You can have a more comfortable experience in the three cinemas at the Caudan Waterfront Complex (U A2) *(map a2)*, where current international films are shown in French-language versions *(Entry 175 rupees)*.

## WHERE TO STAY

### LE LABOURDONNAIS WATERFRONT HOTEL (U A2) *(map a2)*

This elegant business hotel at the harbour is located in the middle of the Caudan Shopping Centre. Rooms start at 12,000 rupees. *108 rooms | Caudan Waterfront | tel. 2 02 40 00 | www.labourdonnais.com | Expensive*

### MON CHOIX (121 E2) *(map D6)*

Southeast of Port Louis, in the Vallée des Prêtres, these ☺ INSIDER TIP eco-lodges are located in the middle of an enormous private park with small streams and beautiful walking routes. An idyllic spot for relaxing and unwinding. *4 rooms/suites | Senneville | Upper Vallée des Prêtres | tel. 7 60 08 36 | www.ecomauritius.com | Budget*

### LE SAINT GEORGES HOTEL (U B4) *(map b4)*

This city hotel is located in the postmodern AAA Tower in the city centre. *59 rooms | 19 Rue Saint Georges | tel. 2 11 25 81 | www.saintgeorgeshotel-mu.com | Moderate*

## INFORMATION

### MAURITIUS TOURISM PROMOTION AUTHORITY (U B4) *(map b4)*

This tourist office is located in Victoria House. *St. Louis Street | tel. 2 10 15 45 | www.tourism-mauritius.mu*

### CHAPELLE SAINTE CROIX
### (121 E1) (*∭ D6*)

The Catholic priest Père Laval, a native of France, came to Mauritius as a missionary in 1841. He campaigned in particular to help the black population and assisted those affected by leprosy. He was revered even during his lifetime and after his death on 9 September 1864 it's said that many miracle cures occurred at his grave, so it's still visited by many people with disabilities. Père Laval was beatified by Pope John Paul II in 1979. Such a great number of believers were making the annual pilgrimage to his chapel and his glass coffin on the anniversary of his death that the building was extended into a large, modern church with a giant forecourt. There's an exhibition about the life of this 'Apostle of Black People' and you can buy souvenirs. *On the northern outskirts of Port Louis, go on the Route de Pamplemousses until the sign that says 'City Boundary'. Then turn towards the mountains down Avenue Père Laval | Church open daily 6.30am–6pm, exhibition and shop 8.30am–noon, as well as 1pm–4.45pm, Sun 10am–noon and 1pm–4.15pm | Free entry*

### DOMAINE LES PAILLES
### (121 D2) (*∭ D6*)

The plantation-style complex was designed as a tourist attraction that relives 19th century life, with an old locomotive steaming through the grounds. In the replica of an ox-powered, 18th century sugar mill, and in a reconstructed rum distillery, the staff wear period costumes and tell you about the various steps of production required to turn sugar cane into sugar and its by-product, rum. Carriage rides are also offered and you can also ride a horse yourself.

The site also boasts a boutique, a souvenir shop, a few restaurants (including one of the top restaurants on the island), a casino and a convention centre. The Domaine Les Pailles is located near the city's southern exit near the motorway. *Entry 1055 rupees, tours through the grounds 355 rupees | tel. 2 86 42 25 | www.domainelespailles.net*

# MOUNTAIN WALKS

From a distance, the mountains **(121 E–F 1–2) (*∭ D6*)** around Port Louis look absolutely spectacular. Most of the peaks, however, can be reached by relatively easy hiking trails. You do have to climb on some of them, however: up to around 820m/2700ft on the *Pieter Both*, which has a distinctive ball-shaped boulder at the top. It's said that as long as the boulder remains up there, all will be well on Mauritius. The climb up *Le Pouce* (811m/2660ft high) is comfortable. Because of the relatively large differences in height, you should set aside a good half day for the hike. The way up starts at St Anne Chapel near the racecourse and takes you through the Vallée de Pouce. From there the path is clearly visible. The hiking trail on the 306m/1004ft-high ⚜ *Priest's Peak* isn't too difficult. The footpath begins near the intersection of the Route Militaire and the Route de Pamplemousses. The climb to the summit takes about an hour.

### EUREKA ★ (121 D3) (*🗺 D7*)

This colonial villa, which is located around 6km/4mi from the southern edge of Port Louis, is a wonderful example of Creole architecture. It was built in 1836, extended in 1856, and remains beautifully preserved to the present day. Decorated with furniture from the 19th century, the first floor's eight bedrooms and one bathroom convey an impression of the stately life of a past era. Photographs from that era are also on display in one of the rooms. In addition, the first floor includes a gallery and a souvenir shop.

Meals for groups of up to 15 diners are served on the long table in the old dining room *(negotiable | from 1800 rupees per person, plus a 6000 Rupee flat rate for the room)*. Creole menus are served to guests on the veranda at lunchtime *(approx. 660 rupees). Mon–Sat 9am–5pm, Sun 9am–3pm | Moka | Montagne Ory (the route is signposted from the motorway) | Entry to the museum, 175 rupees. Entry to the waterfall area and the house, 300 rupees | tel. 433 8477 | www.maisoneureka.com*

### KALAISSON TEMPLE ★
(121 E1) (*🗺 D6*)

This large, colourful temple complex of the southern Indian Tamil people, located in the Abercrombie district (not far from the Chapel of Saint Croix), gives an insight into the fascinating world of the Hindu gods. A high gopuram (a tower gate that grants access to the temple), decorated with figures, adorns the main hall in which the larger-than-life statues of gods with multiple arms and faces stare (often quite grimly) at visitors. Before visiting, you must leave your shoes at the door because the temple complex may only be entered barefoot. Photography is allowed. If you follow the Route de

Statue in the Tamil Kalaisson Temple

Pamplemousses through Abercrombie in a northerly direction, you'll notice a beige-coloured temple complex on the right hand side. A few hundred metres beyond this, the brightly coloured Kalaisson Temple rises up on the right-hand side. It's easily visible from the mountains of the Montagne Longue. *Daily 8am–6pm | Free entry*

# THE EAST

**Pointe Quatre Cocos is the island's easternmost point and is regarded by locals as the end of the world. When they want to say how foolish someone is, they say 'Il vient de Quatre Cocos' – 'He comes from Quatre Cocos'.**

It's a poor area where inhabitants live from fishing and agriculture and in particular with the cultivation of sugar cane, the history of which dates back to the time of the Dutch settlers. These first inhabitants settled on the flat plains, called 'flacq', and began to cultivate fields very early on. Even today, the largest sugar factory on the island is located in the east, although the practice of agricultural monoculture brings prosperity only to very few. When you see women washing their clothes in the streams and leaving them to dry over bushes, it might seem like an idyllic scene for holidaymakers, but it's actually only an indication of poverty. The people here are steeped in tradition. The few towns in the east offer a rather bleak picture. Unlike on the west coast, where European fashion long ago determined what's worn on the streets, many women here wear saris.

A light breeze always blows across the country and along the coast, making the sea here a paradise for windsurfers and sailors. The region is traversed by the Montagne Bambous mountain range, which reaches right to the sea in the east. The road follows the winding route of the stony coast. There aren't any bathing beaches in the far south because there's a gap here in the Mauritian coral reef.

Photo: Île aux Cerfs

A world apart: the region is much less developed and is poorer than the rest of the island. It's still possible to meet Mauritians on the beaches

The east is becoming increasingly developed for tourism with the appearance of luxury hotels along the beaches. At weekends, however, the locals still come here and there's a great hustle and bustle as picnic baskets are unpacked and sega and reggae ring out from ghetto blasters.

**sparkling water.**
From the main road on, there's a seemingly endless number of small roads that branch off and go down through the filao groves to small swimming bays. A carnival atmosphere reigns along the *Plage de Palmar* at weekends.

# BELLE MARE

(123 E3) *(ᗉ H6)* **This place takes its name from the area's exceptionally**

## FOOD & DRINK

SYMON'S RESTAURANT
An eatery with an open veranda located on the coastal road. The specialities are

seafood and Creole dishes. *Daily | Pointe de Flacq | tel. 4 15 11 35 | Budget*

## WHERE TO STAY

### BELLE MARE PLAGE

This resort combines casual elegance, luxury villas with butler service, and a beautiful sandy beach. The 235 rooms

### LE SAINT GÉRAN

This well-kept traditional hotel is one of the best beach resorts in the world and is situated on a small, lush peninsula. Special features include the *Spoon des Îles* restaurant, run by the Parisian star chef Alain Ducasse, an ultra modern fitness centre, a casino, and a 9-hole golf course. Rooms from 16,000 rupees. *175*

You can put your skills to the test on the golf course at Belle Mare Plage

and suites are spread over several buildings in a tropical garden. **INSIDER TIP** The hotel's own golf courses *Links* and *Legend* are both a challenge – even for low handicappers (18 holes, par 72). *tel. 4 02 26 00 | www.bellemareplagehotel.com | Expensive*

### EMERAUDE HOTEL

A simple but beautiful hotel that's only separated from a magnificent beach and a lagoon by a narrow street. There are two swimming pools. Ideal for divers and kitesurfers. *61 rooms | tel. 4 01 14 00 | Moderate*

*rooms | tel. 4 01 16 88 | lesaintgeran.one andonlyresorts.com | Expensive*

## SPORTS & ACTIVITIES

### LE WATERPARK & LEISURE VILLAGE

A theme park with lots of pools and all sorts of spectacular slides that will delight children and adults alike. Start with the 'Lazy River' and let yourself drift comfortably through this resort and its many caves. *Open daily in summer, 10am–6pm, in winter 10am–5.30pm | Entry 350 rupees, children 185 rupees | www.lewaterpark.intnet.mu*

# CENTRE DE FLACQ & POSTE DE FLACQ

**(123 D2–3) (ill G6) The name 'Flacq' is derived from the Dutch word 'vlak' meaning 'flat land'. There are two places that bear this name: a small provincial town in the interior of the country, and Poste de Flacq which is situated 5.5km/3.5mi further to the northeast.**

This town is home to the Hindu Temple of *Sagar Shir Mandir*, which is well worth seeing because of its location on a tiny peninsula.

Centre de Flacq is a typical small Mauritian town in which a predominantly Indian population lives. The main street is fittingly named *Market Road* and there are shops and stalls as far as the eye can see. On Sundays, the hustle and bustle reaches its height and you'll find the INSIDER TIP market taking place around the District Court. Clothes, materials, fruit and vegetables are all on offer.

By appointment, it's possible to have a tour of the *F.U.E.L. sugar factory (tel. 4 02 33 00)* between June and November. There's a surprise in store for many visitors: the factory consumes a quarter of the island's electricity needs. So, to generate energy they burn bagasse, a waste product that's left over after the cane's pressed. This material's also used to fertilise the fields.

## FOOD & DRINK

### INSIDER TIP CHEZ MANUEL

An out-of-the-way Chinese restaurant. The specialities include sweet and sour fish with ginger, and pork in honey. *Mon–Sat | 8km/5mi southwest of Centre de Flacq in St Julien | Royal Road | Union Flacq | tel. 4 18 35 99 | Moderate*

## WHERE TO STAY

### LA MAISON D'ÉTÉ

A pretty bungalow complex for self-caterers located away from villages and towns. A small restaurant, pool and boathouse are all included. *10 bungalows | approx. 10 km/6mi north of Poste de Flacq on the coast | tel. 4 10 50 39 | www.lamaisondete.com | Budget–Moderate*

### LE PRINCE MAURICE

One of the top three hotels on the island. Situated on a peninsula, this hotel, built from valuable natural materials and decorated in discreet colours, looks as if it sim-

---

### ⭐ Excursions
Between the mountain ranges of the Montagne Fayence and Montagne Blanche there's a tropical world just waiting to be explored → p. 62

### ⭐ Kestrel Valley
Great for hunters, nature lovers and a good destination for foodies → p. 65

### ⭐ Le Val
A small nature park with greenhouses and a zoo. Come and stroll on through! → p. 66

### ⭐ Île aux Cerfs
White sand lapped by crystal clear water: Mauritius' most beautiful beach is found on this small bathing island → p. 67

**MARCO POLO HIGHLIGHTS**

ply grew out of the landscape. It's luxurious: the bathrooms are as large as the bedrooms, and many suites have their own pool. The complex consists of three very good à la carte restaurants, two bars, a library and a fitness centre. Guests are entitled to play golf on the course at the Hotel Belle Mare Plage. Rooms cost from 16,000 rupees. *89 Suites | Choisy Road | Poste de Flacq | tel. 4023636 | www. princemaurice.com | Expensive*

## WHERE TO GO

### BEL AIR (123 E4) (*ØØ G7*)

This small town, located 8km/5mi to the south of Centre de Flacq provides the starting point for a delightful ★ *excursion* around the ﾟ *Montagne Blanche* (532m/1745ft), the *Montagne Fayence* (433m/1421ft) and finally down to *Camp de Masque* (122 C4) (*ØØ F7*). The only attraction in Bel Air is the colourful temple of *Siva Soopramaniarkovil*, located in the

middle of a sugar cane field at the western exit of the town. During the onward journey to Clemencia, the beauty of nature excels itself, with banana plants, hibiscus, palms, eucalyptus and flowers in all colours thriving here.

# MAHÉBOURG

**(127 D3)** (*ØØ F–G10*) **Mahébourg was once the second most important city on the island. Today it's a sleepy provincial town with just under 20,000 inhabitants.** When a malaria epidemic broke out in the 19th century the survivors fled to and settled in this higher region. The central point of the town is the bus station. From here you can reach the *Rue Flamant* shopping street. You can also just as easily reach the park that lies along the bay, which was, in 1810, the site of the most important naval battle off the coast of Mauritius.

## SIGHTSEEING

### CATHEDRAL

*Notre Dame des Anges*, built in 1849 in the English neo-Gothic style, is worth a look because of the impressive ceiling construction with its 20 individually carved angels. The door to the ﾟ tower, which has a view over the bay at Grand Port, is sometimes open. *Royal Road*

### INSIDER TIP ▶ NATIONAL HISTORY MUSEUM

A naval museum in an 18th century mansion. The exhibits mainly document the naval war between France and England. The attractions include wreckage from the battle of 1810, a model of the 'St Géran' and one of the trains that used to travel across the island from 1864 to 1926. In addition, you can also see colonial furniture and cannon. In the garden, crafts people can be seen in their workshops. *Royal Road | Mon, Wed–Sat 9am–4pm, Sun 9am–noon | Free entry*

### PARK

There's a row of monuments on the promenade, which has lots of picnic spots. An inconspicuous obelisk commemorates the victims of a shipwreck in

road to Blue Bay. *Daily | Pointe d'Esny | tel. 6 31 58 01 | Budget–Moderate*

### LES COPAINS D'ABORD

A beautiful restaurant right by the sea. Specialities include seafood and wild game. *Daily | Rue Shivanada | tel. 6 31 97 28 | Moderate*

The weekly market in Mahébourg offers an insight into daily life on Mauritius.

1874. A larger monument is dedicated to the English and French soldiers who lost their lives in the battle near Île de la Passe in 1810. The nearly 6m-high likeness of Buddha, the *Statue of Harmony*, is remarkable. *Directly next to the Bay of Mahébourg*

### TEMPLE

The Tamil temple of *Shri Vinayaour Seedalamen* was built in 1856 and is found directly next to the main street. The complex consists of several large and small temples. *Daily 6am–noon and 3.30pm–6pm*

## FOOD & DRINK

### BLUE BAMBOO

A charming Creole garden restaurant with an extensive menu, located on the

### LE JARDIN DE BEAU VALLON

Mauritian specialities, served in the ambience of a colonial house on the edge of a sugar cane field. *Daily | travelling in the direction of the airport, it's located right in front of the entrance to the town of Mahébourg | tel. 6 31 28 50 | Moderate*

### LA VIEILLE ROUGE

This restaurant is very popular with the locals because of its fish and seafood. Ask about the catch of the day! *Daily | On the corner of Colony and Souffleur Street, near the church | tel. 6 31 39 80 | Budget*

## SHOPPING

On Mondays there's a colourful weekly market spread all along Rue Hollandaise.

It's primarily aimed at locals, which makes it a great attraction for tourists.

### CASSAVA COOKIE FACTORY ●

This cookie factory has been family-owned since 1870. Now in its fourth generation, cookies are made out of the cassava root based on an old recipe and with authentic equipment. Today, however, they also have a wider selection on offer, with some cookies infused with

armed bandits and at the tables. *Daily 10am–4am | Rue Labourdonnais (near the market) | tel. 6 31 29 90*

## WHERE TO STAY

### AUBERGE AQUARELLA

A charming family hotel on the sea with clean rooms. A good restaurant with a few tables and a sunny terrace. The nearest beach is a just a few miles away at

Gorgeous scenery: Île aux Aigrettes is a sanctuary for endangered species.

vanilla, coconut and chocolate. It's worth trying some of these delicacies here with a cup of coffee or, as tradition would have it, a cup of tea. *Biscuiterie Rault | Ville Noire, Mahébourg | Mon–Fri 9am–3pm | tel. 6 31 95 59*

## SPORTS & ACTIVITIES

The most beautiful beach in Mahébourg is located on the INSIDER TIP *Pointe Jerôme*. Surfers will find ideal conditions here.

## ENTERTAINMENT

The *Senator* casino offers entertainment. You can try your luck here on the one-

Blue Bay. *9 rooms | Sivananda Road | tel. 6 31 27 67 | Budget*

### INSIDER TIP LE BARACHOIS

For people who like something a bit different. The 16 rooms of this hotel are located in a natural stone house with a thatched roof and shutters instead of windows. It's decorated with Creole furniture. The hotel is situated in the middle of a lagoon and is surrounded by oyster and shrimp farms and a mangrove forest. There's an excellent restaurant. *18km/11mi north of Mahébourg, after Bambous Virieux on the lagoon | tel. 6 34 56 43 | Moderate*

## LA HACIENDA

These four lodges are located right in the middle of natural surroundings on the slopes of the Montagne du Lion, next to the Vallée de Ferney Nature Reserve. The houses all have a kitchen, one or two bedrooms and a terrace, and are set in a private garden with a view of the south coast and the sea. Ideal for holidaymakers seeking peace and quiet. *Vieux Grand Port | www.lahaciendamauritius.com | Budget–Moderate*

## PARADISE BEACH

This property with eight apartments and two penthouses can be found in *Pointe d'Esny* right next to a sandy beach. All of them are luxuriously furnished down to the last detail. They haven't missed a trick: there's even a grill on the balconies and terraces. Guests can share a pool in the small tropical garden. *Tel. 4 52 10 10 | www.horizon.mu | Moderate–Expensive*

## SHANDRANI

Here, the sometimes frowned-upon all-inclusive concept is offered at a luxury level. Five restaurants offer great variety. The hotel includes a spa and has many activities on offer, such as diving and golf. The complex is surrounded by three beaches. The islands of the Blue Bay Nature Park with its magnificent underwater world is only a short boat ride away. *327 rooms | Blue Bay | tel. 6 03 43 43 | www.shandrani-resort.com | Expensive*

## WHERE TO GO

### BLUE BAY (127 D4) (*Ø G10*)

A bay to the south of Mahébourg with a bathing beach, which can be reached at the end of the peninsula. Locals populate the bay on Sundays and on holidays. From here you can climb aboard a glass-bottomed boat from which you can ex-plore the marine park, marvel at beautiful coral formations and go snorkelling. The service providers are numerous (see the 'Low Budget' box).

### INSIDER TIP ÎLE AUX AIGRETTES
(127 E3) (*Ø G10*)

The Mauritian Wildlife Fund is replanting the original coastal forests of Mauritius here. The 25 hectare-large island is already home to many species of endangered animals and plants. In the long term they're even planning to reintroduce land-dwelling tortoises. At the *Visitor Centre* you can learn about the over-exploitation and destruction of the environment. There are guided nature tours every day lasting two to three hours. The tours cost 800 rupees including the ferry ride. Book through local tour operators or by *phone, tel. 2 58 81 39.*

### KESTREL VALLEY ★ (127 D–E1) (*Ø G9*)

Fantastic for nature lovers, hikers and hunters, and also for day-trippers who want to eat well surrounded by lush vegetation. After around a 20-minute drive, turn north of Mahébourg near Anse Jonchée (the former name of the *Domaine d'Anse Jonchée*). You'll arrive in this green mountain landscape, home to deer, monkeys and wild boar. Walking trips and jeep tours are offered that take you to a 🔍 viewing point *(prices differ depending on the program)*. It's also possible to go hunting on the property or to accompany a hunter on the prowl *(for a surcharge)*. The estate *(Expensive)* has two restaurants and six small chalets *tel. 6 34 50 97 | ledomaine@intnet.mu*

### MONTAGNE DU LION (127 E1) (*Ø G9*)

If you come from the south, the Montagne du Lion actually resembles a reclining lion. The tour up to the 480m/1575ft-high summit begins in the village of Vieux

# MAHÉBOURG

Grand Port. It should only be undertaken by experienced hikers because you'll have to overcome a few difficult passages. The view over the sea, which spreads out below in various shades ranging from blue to turquoise, makes the ascent up the mountain unforgettable.

### LE SOUFFLEUR (126 C5) *(ⱷ F11)*
Here you can take one of the few opportunities to reach the rugged cliffs of the south coast by car. *Access by a side road at L'Escalier.*

### LE VAL ★ (126 C2) *(ⱷ E9)*
This small nature park is a great destination for lunch. It lies 12km/7mi northwest of Mahébourg beyond St Hubert. If you're in the mood to eat, order soon after you arrive and take a walk over the grounds to the deer enclosures, the giant tortoises, the greenhouses and the carp pond. There's also a playground. *Daily 9am–5pm | Entry 50 rupees*

In *Le Val* restaurant everything comes from their own garden. You can catch your fish yourself. *Daily 9am–3pm | Reservation recommended | tel. 6 33 60 58 | Moderate*

### VIEUX GRAND PORT (127 D2) *(ⱷ G9)*
This was once the most important harbour on the island. The defensive complex and the remains of a tower reveal the distant history of the place. The *Frederik Hendrik Museum* gives an overview *(Royal Road | Wed–Mon 9am–4pm | Free entry)* and is stocked with old engravings and archaeological finds. The graveyard of the first Dutch settlers is also worth a look *(Cemetery Road)*.

### YLANG YLANG (127 E1) *(ⱷ G9)*
Essential oils are distilled on this plantation, which now belongs to the Kestrel Valley complex. Their oils form the basis

# BOOKS & FILMS

▶ **Paul and Virginie** – A couple is destroyed by their own ideals, and there isn't a more famous story on Mauritius. The book by Jacques-Henri Bernardin de Saint-Pierre appeared in 1788. Today, it takes a taste for kitsch to enjoy its heavy melodrama.

▶ **The Rape of Sita** – This prize-winning novel by Lindsey Collen about a rape was banned in Mauritius. It can be bought in bookshops at home, however.

▶ **The Dodo on Mauritius** – For this photo book, the Finnish conceptual artist and photographer Harri Kallio used bird models to create lavish, lovingly created scenes that display an avian idyll that existed before the arrival of the first human beings.

▶ **My Father the Hero** – In this 1991 comedy, filmed in Mauritius, Gérard Depardieu, in the role of a father on holiday, has to realise that is teenage daughter is more interested in young men than in him.

▶ **Gor (1987)** – Jack Palance and Oliver Reed take the leading roles in this outrageous story about a professor who's sent to another dimension by a magical ring. At least they got something right: the scenery.

of well-known perfumes. If you make an arrangement in advance *(tel. 6 34 50 97)*, it's possible to take a tour of the distillery. Walking trails lead through the complex *(2.5km/1.5mi | 50 rupees)* and there are also jeep safari tours on offer *(prices depend on the tour | tel. 6 34 50 11)*. There's a beautiful view to be had from the ☆ restaurant *(Moderate)*. *Daily 9am–5pm | Anse Jonchée | Vieux Grand Port*

# TROU D'EAU DOUCE

**(123 E4) *(ꭍ H7)* Trou d'Eau Douce is a fishing village with a small harbour situated in a beautiful bay.**
There's a large church built of volcanic rock in the village. The men of the village meet in the tiny *Victoria Square* to play boules.

*al Road | tel. 4 80 13 00 | www.attitude resorts.com | Moderate*

Giant tortoises make their home in Le Val Nature Park

## WHERE TO STAY

### LE TOUESSROK
The complex, partially located on an island, is built in the style of a Mediterranean village. There are boat shuttles to the hotel's own 'Desert Island' and to Île aux Cerfs, on which Bernhard Langer has created an 18-hole golf course that's also open to non-residents. Room prices from 16,000 rupees. *200 rooms | tel. 4 02 74 00 | www.letouessrokresort.com | Expensive*

### LE TROPICAL
A small, family-friendly, all-inclusive hotel that lies next to the beach at Trou d'Eau Douce and comes complete with a pool. The bungalows' Creole architecture fits in perfectly with the island's tropical natural beauty. *60 rooms | Coast-*

## WHERE TO GO

### ÎLE AUX CERFS ★ ☆
**(123 F4–5) *(ꭍ H7–8)***
Mauritius' best-loved bathing island impresses visitors with its white beaches. A small part of the island, right on the pier, is managed by the nearby Hotel *Le Touessrok (a bar, and two restaurants serving snacks and Mauritian cuisine | Moderate)*. There are numerous water sports on offer and a public golf course designed by Bernhard Langer. ● As soon as you leave this rather busy part of the island, you'll think you're completely alone. The Île aux Cerfs can be reached by boat between 9am and 5pm. The journey lasts approximately 15 minutes. *Round trip approx. 400 rupees | Departure points on the beach at Trou d'Eau Douce*

# THE SOUTH WEST

**The area is wild and untouched – it's the only region on the island that gives an idea of how Mauritius probably looked before the settlers landed here and began to clear away the jungle.**
Steep cliffs, deep gorges, roaring waterfalls and an impenetrable jungle complete the picture. If you can tear yourself away from the comfort of your hotel for just one day of your holiday, you should come here.

The south west boasts two superlatives: it has the island's greatest amount of rainfall, and the Black River peak is the island's highest mountain (828m/2717ft). You can find an abundance of flora in this region and the remote location, Mauritius' only national park, offers a safe haven for wildlife. Some of the rare pink pigeons and the Mauritian kestrel still make this part of the island their home. Despite the region's untouched appearance, people have been settling here since the 19th century: black people, who turned their backs on the white world after the abolition of slavery, came here and founded their own villages. Some huts look as if they're made of driftwood; the small plots of land outside serve simultaneously as fruit and vegetable gardens, a scratching ground for chickens and as a pasture for a goat or a cow.

Fishing villages are lined up on the narrow strip between the mountains and the sea. In the south, where the coral reef is interrupted, violent waves crash against the beaches. Unpredictable currents also make swimming dangerous,

Photo: Terres des Sept Couleurs in Chamarel

Rare plants and animals, deep canyons and striking mountains: in this region you can see the island as it was before settlers arrived

meaning that there aren't any beach hotels here. In the west, it's the usual scenario, however: calm water, white beaches, filao groves and the largest port for deep-sea fishing on the island.

# CHAMAREL

(124 C3) (*ℳ B10*) **Once a year, during Assumption on 15 August, this small creole village turns into a veritable fairground.**

On this day believers flock to *Saint Anne Chapel*. With them come vendors and food stalls. The village is surrounded by coffee and sugar cane plantations.

## SIGHTSEEING

### CASCADE CHAMAREL
These 90m/295ft-high twin waterfalls, over which the water from the Rivière de Cap plummets, can be found near the village. You can enjoy the impressive view from a viewing platform.

# CHAMAREL

The reward after a hard climb: the view from Black River Peak

### TERRES DES SEPT COULEURS

Charamel is known for its coloured earth. The undulating ground spreads over approximately one hectare. The main colour is a rusty red. Depending on the time of day, the layers of earth can look yellow, orange, blue or even purple, though there's no clear scientific explanation for why this happens. The hilly landscape is supposed to be volcanic in origin and is said to have been caused by mineral oxidation. *Park grounds daily 7.30am–5.30pm | Entry approx. 125 rupees*

FOOD & DRINK

### LE CHAMAREL ⊗

A restaurant with great views and good Creole cuisine. The speciality is wild game. After the meal they serve coffee grown in Mauritius. *Daily | La Crête | Chamarel | tel. 4 83 64 21 | Moderate–Expensive*

### VARANGUE SUR MORNE ★

This former banana and pineapple plantation overseer's house is situated on the road to Mare aux Vacoas. From the ⊗ veranda there's a great view of the mountains. It's popular with tourist groups. *Mon–Sat | 110 Route de Plaine Champagne | tel. 4 83 57 10 | Moderate–Expensive*

WHERE TO GO

### GRAND BASSIN ● ⊗
### (125 E3) (*∅ C10*)

Although the name would suggest the opposite, Grand Bassin is only a small like, situated less than 20km/12mi east of Charamel. This extinct volcano vent is famous because of the *Maha Shivaratree Festival*. Each year in February/March, over 300,000 Hindus make a pilgrimage to this holy place. Small temples and altars are located on the shore. You can't miss the 35m/115ft-high Shri Mangal Mahadev Statue, built in 2005. *Daily 6am–6pm | Free entry*

### LE PÉTRIN AND THE PLAINE CHAMPAGNE (125 D–E3) (*∅ C10*)

The *Black River Gorge* National Park is located in the deep gorge of the 'black river'. Its centrepiece, however, is the

749m/2547ft-high barren plateau, the *Plaine Champagne*. A narrow road wends its way through the area, and tracks branch off and lead to viewing points over gorges and waterfalls, the most beautiful being the 🔆 view of the *Black River Waterfall* at *Le Pétrin*. The approx. 16km/10mi-long winding drive from Le Pétrin over the *Chemin Grenier* to the *Rivière des Galets*, past the remarkable *Vallée des 23 Couleurs (125 E4) (㎞ C10)*, is well worth the trip. It takes you through high forests and pineapple plantations and offers views of the south coast's rough shore. When you get there, you arrive back on the main road on the island's southernmost tip.

# GRANDE RI-VIÈRE NOIRE

(124 B–C2) (㎞ B9) **Professional deep-sea anglers gather here in the high season from March to November.**

They organise competitions and pull heavy blue marlin (up to 650kg/1433lb) and other fish out of the water. A six-hour excursion costs around 10,000 rupees. The inhabitants of this town, mainly Creoles, are among the poorest of the island's inhabitants. But this has no harmful effect at all on their love of life. The streets are always busy and are often filled with spontaneous parties, particularly at weekends.

## WHERE TO GO

**BLACK RIVER GORGES NATIONAL PARK**
★ (124–125 C–E 2–4) (㎞ B–C 9–10)
Several protected nature reserves have been merged together to create this park. At 66 km²/41mi², it occupies 3.5 per cent of the island's total surface area. The land-scape ranges from the summit of the 828m/2717ft-high *Black River Peak*, the island's tallest mountain, down to the thick rainforest that grows along the steep slopes of the *Savanne Mountains*. 150 native plants and nine endangered species of bird can only be found in this park.

The route through the *Macchabée Tropical Forest* and the INSIDER TIP *Black River Gorges* is particularly worthwhile. From 🔆 *Black River Peak (Piton de la Petite Rivière Noire)* you can out see over the whole island. A hiking path begins near the viewing point in the National Park, but take note that it's very slippery after rain. The trail is easy at first but it becomes increasingly demanding. The last part is heavy going and has difficult sections. It almost

---

seems as if the final 20m up to the summit go vertically. You're rewarded, however, with a fantastic view. In clear weather you can even see the island of Réunion on the horizon. If you don't feel safe alone in the mountains, Yan is a reliable guide *(tel. 785 6177 | www.yanature.com)*.

The *Visitor Centre (tel. 464 40 16)* in the National Park will tell you (rather perfunctorily) about the park's flora and fauna. As it often rains in the afternoon, you should visit the area as early in the day as possible.

# LE MORNE BRABANT

**(124 A4) (*𝄞 A10*) The prominent mountain of Le Morne Brabant (556 m/1824ft) is located on a peninsula. It was listed as a Unesco World Heritage Site in 2008, prompted by the mountain's connection with the history of the slave trade.**

In the 19th century the mountains were the site of a tragic misunderstanding. During French rule, runaway slaves used the slopes of the mountain as a hiding place. When the English had abolished slavery and policemen were sent to tell people about their newfound freedom, they believed themselves to be discovered and threw themselves in desperation to their deaths.

Today, there's a memorial here to commemorate the tragic event. On 1 February, the festival commemorating the abolition of slavery, many come here to have a picnic. Bands play and there's singing and dancing.

Windsurfers and kitesurfers meet at the southwest tip of the island, on the beach of Le Morne Brabant, to surf at the *Big Eye*.

## FOOD & DRINK

**LE SIROKAN (124 B3) (*𝄞 A–B10*)**
Creole-Indian restaurant where you can get good fish dishes. *Daily | La Gaulette | Royal Road | tel. 451 51 15 | Moderate*

## WHERE TO STAY

**DINAROBIN HOTEL GOLF & SPA ★ ●**
**(124 A4) (*𝄞 A10*)**
This resort, with the spectacular Le Morne mountain in the background, is a place of peace and quiet that's ideal for

The surf in front of Morne Brabant – a dream for kitesurfers and windsurfers

relaxation. The complex boasts pools on many levels, a terraces overlooking the sea, and a garden, all of which make it the very picture of tropical elegance. Guests can use all of the facilities at the neighbouring Paradis hotel, including the 18-hole golf course (par 72). Rooms from 12,000 rupees. *172 Suites | Le Morne Peninsula | tel. 4 01 49 00 | www. dinarobin-hotel.com | Expensive*

### LUX* LE MORNE (124 A4) (𝄔 A10)

Situated between the majestic Le Morne mountain and a beautiful beach with snorkelling locations, this five-star resort is dripping in tropical style. The hotel boasts 149 luxurious suites with balconies or terraces, and four restaurants. *Le Morne Plage | tel. 4 01 40 00 | www.naia de.com | Expensive*

### ROPSEN TOUR OPERATOR (124 B3) (𝄔 A–B10)

Ropsen offers simple but very clean apartments for self-caterers. Ideal for surfers, and those who want to have plenty of contact with the locals. *La Gaulette | Royal Road | tel. 4 51 57 63 | Budget–Moderate*

## WHERE TO GO

### BEL OMBRE ☼ (124 C5) (𝄔 B11)

It's worth making the trip along the coast from Le Morne Brabant through the colourful Creole village of Baie du Cap and on to Bel Ombre. The area has been developed for tourism through the building of four luxury resorts *(Le Telfair, Heritage Golf & Spa, Mövenpick, Tamassa Hotel)* and a golf course. You can go hiking and zip lining from tree to tree in *Chazal* which is flanked on the south by the National Park *(tel. 4 22 31 17)*

Continue on the ★ *Coastal road to Souillac* which takes you through a landscape of undulating hills, past fishing boats, colourful houses and small Creole shops.

### INSIDER TIP ▶ ÎLE AUX BÉNITIERS (124 B3) (𝄔 A10)

A bathing island in a turquoise lagoon. Boat connections set off from the Hotel Le Paradis. The farmers on the island were once the island's main suppliers of coconuts.

# SOUILLAC

**(125 F5–6) (𝄔 D11) This fishing village boasts a natural harbour.**

The village itself consists of little more than a disproportionately large bus station, a church, a Hindu temple, a park and a few shops.

## SIGHTSEEING

### GRIS GRIS ● ☼

This is a vantage point at the southern end of the village. The coast is wild here and the sea thrashes against the rocks, making bathing lethal. The availability of parking and refreshments has made Gris Gris a meeting place. You can also get a beautiful view of the waves a little further on from *La roche qui pleure*, the 'crying rock'.

## MUSÉE ROBERT EDWARD HART ●

This was once the refuge of Mauritian poet Robert Edward Hart who died here in 1954 at the age of 63. Hart was born in Port Louis and was initially a journalist and librarian before he started to write the poems and novels for which he was honoured by the Académie Française. His house and the museum are located right next to the sea on the way to Gris Gris. You can see his furniture, portraits of the poet and his publications. *Mon/Wed 9am–2pm, Thu/Fri 9am–4pm, Sat/Sun 9am–noon | Free entry*

## ROCHESTER FALLS ●

If you ask the boys on the northern outskirts of the village the way to these waterfalls, they'll answer with a mysterious 'très compliqué'. They then offer to lead the way and to go ahead of you by bike – for a price. In truth, there are very few signs pointing out the route. You should negotiate your price with the guide be-

# LOW BUDGET

▶ *Le Kiosk Bar* in the Ruisseau Créole shopping centre is the meeting point in Rivière Noire. Drinks and snacks are available until late at night. The guests are a mixture of Mauritians and Europeans. *Tel. 4 83 70 04*

▶ Sega and reggae are played on the beach and spontaneous concerts often take place on Saturday evenings. The hotels can often give advice and an overview can be found on: *www. radiomoris.com*

fore starting your drive. Although the water of the Rochester Falls only plummets from a height of 15m, the surrounding landscape makes this an idyllic spot.

## FOOD & DRINK

### LE BATELAGE

This small Creole restaurant is situated in an idyllic location on the estuary by the harbour. *Daily | tel. 6 25 60 83 | Budget–Moderate*

### INSIDER TIP ST-AUBIN TABLE D'HÔTE

If you book ahead you can enjoy a Creole lunch menu in this mansion, built in 1819. A tour of the house, gardens and the vanilla farm rounds off the visit. A visit to this place is highly recommended! *Daily | Rivière des Anguilles | Royal Road | tel. 6 26 15 13 | Moderate*

## WHERE TO STAY

### CHALETS CHAZAL ☺ (125 D5) (*m* C11)

Built in a mix of colonial and Creole styles, the complex's six chalets are surrounded by sugar cane plantations and wild nature. Each house has a terrace and a small garden. Power is provided by solar energy and turbines. The water comes from a spring. Vegetables are harvested daily from their large garden, prepared in the kitchen, and served in their own restaurant. Depending on the season, you can also treat yourself to freshly picked exotic fruit. You can also bathe in the rivers and in a natural pool in the grounds. *Impasse de La Forêt | Chamouny | tel. 6 22 21 48 | www.incentivepart nersltd.com | Moderate*

### SHANTI MAURICE (125 D5) (*m* C11)

Originally a luxury spa, this resort is now also open to families. The focus is on the Ayerveda tradition and everything is bespoke, from the treatments to the cooking. If you'd rather have something less ascetic, you can also choose from the refined à la carte menu. There aren't any buffets, not even for breakfast: every need is fulfilled individually. There's a very beautiful beach. Rooms from 12,000 rupees. *55 rooms, some bungalows, one presidential villa | Chemin Grenier | tel. 6 03 72 00 | www.shantimaurice.com | Expensive*

earth shone in 23 shimmering colours, including grey, blue, red and violet – a geological sensation that turned his fruit and vegetable business into a tourist destination. There are two trails with numerous small waterfalls, the pools of which you can swim in. *Around 10km/6mi northwest of Souillac: from Chemin Grenier go in the direction of Mont Blanc, then it's signposted | daily*

Muscle instead of machines: women harvesting tea on the Bois Chéri plantation

## WHERE TO GO

### INSIDER TIP BOIS CHÉRI
**(125 F3) (∅ D10)**
On this tea plantation, located 20km/12mi to the north, there's a small museum that explains the cultivation, production and refinement of the beverage. A tea tasting session is included in your visit. *Mon–Fri 8.30am–3.30pm, Sat 8.30am–1pm | Entry 375 rupees | tel. 6 17 91 09*

### INSIDER TIP VALLÉE DES 23 COULEURS
**(125 E4) (∅ C10)**
During construction work in 1998, this plantation's owner discovered that the

*9am–5pm | Entry 200 rupees | tel. 2 92 88 41*

### LA VANILLE RÉSERVE DES MASCAREIGNES (126 A5) (∅ D11)
This park, located in the predominantly Indian *Rivière des Anguilles*, 7km/4mi northeast of Souillac, is well signposted. As well as crocodiles, you can also see monkeys, giant tortoises, small reptiles and a large collection of insects. The restaurant *(tel. 6 26 25 03 | Moderate)* makes its mark with its homemade produce. *Daily 9.30am–5pm | Entry 270 rupees*

# THE WEST

The beaches in the west stretch from Flic en Flac to Tamarin, the best surfing spot on the island. In the hinterland the towns spread out for great distances across the plateau. Founded in the 19th century as independent settlements, these towns have gradually become seamlessly joined together. Attractions for tourists include shopping centres and factory outlets. Colonial villas nestle in lush gardens and tea's grown in the southern highlands.

# CUREPIPE & FLORÉAL

(121 D–E5) (*ɯ D8*) **When malaria broke out in Port Louis and Mahébourg, who-** ever could afford fled the highlands (540m/1770ft) with its healthy climate, and this is how Curepipe was founded. With 65,000 inhabitants, it's one of the largest towns on the island and is regarded by many as the unofficial capital, because important public authorities and radio and television stations have made it their home. The town also boasts the best school, the Royal College, and a sophisticated casino. The rich live in the elegant suburb of Floréal and some of the colonial villas also house embassies.

## SIGHTSEEING

**INSIDER TIP ▶ BOTANICAL GARDEN**

Although much smaller than the garden at Pamplemousses, this park has just as

**Whether in the antique shops, the shopping centres or the markets, the metropolitan area offers many possibilities for shopping and browsing**

much charm. It's a meeting point for young lovers. *Free entry.*

### DOMAINE DES AUBINEAUX
One of the most beautiful manor houses on the island is at Curepipe. The last owner, Louise-Myriam Harel, lived in this villa (built in 1872) until 1999. The décor of the rooms remains almost untouched. You can take a 30-minute tour followed by a tea tasting session. *Mon–Sat 9am–5pm | Entry 300 rupees | Forest Side | tel. 6 76 30 89*

### ST HÉLÈNE CHURCH
A basilica with beautiful windows. With a little bit of luck you'll find the stairs to the ⚶ tower open. *Royal Road | At the exit to the town, travelling in the direction of Phoenix*

### ST THÉRÈSE CHURCH
A three-aisled Roman Catholic church in neo-Gothic style. It boasts an impressive ceiling. *Royal Road*

This volcano hasn't been active for a long time: the crater at Trou aux Cerfs

### TOWN HALL

Old English colonial house (built in 1890) with a tower and a spiral staircase at each corner. Opposite *St Thérèse, near Carnegie Library | Royal Road*

### TOWN HALL GARDENS

A small park behind the town hall in which you can find Prosper d'Epinay's 'Paul et Virginie' bronze statue.

### TROU AUX CERFS ★ ☼

This 650m/2130ft-high volcanic crater gives both an insight into the island's geological history and a view over the whole of Mauritius. With a bit of luck, you'll also be able to see the neighbouring island of Réunion, 170km/105mi away. A marshy habitat has formed in the 85m-deep crater and it's surrounded by a grove. The road runs in a wide circle along the crater's edge.

### FOOD & DRINK

#### LA CLÉF DES CHAMPS

This restaurant will greet you with French cuisine and a charming ambience, all in a Provençale style. Reservation is recommended. *Mon–Fri | Queen Mary Avenue | Floréal | tel. 6 86 34 58 | Moderate–Expensive*

#### GINGER BANANA LEAF

A small eatery in the *Garden Village shopping centre*. Employees come here from offices and banks at midday. European-orientated cooking. *Mon–Sat | Sir Winston Churchill Street | Budget*

#### LA POTINIÈRE

This restaurant has a certain rustic elegance. Specialities include seafood and palm heart salad. *Mon–Sat | Sir Winston Churchill Street | in the Hillcrest Building | tel. 4 92 27 12 | Moderate–Expensive*

### SHOPPING

Curepipe is the best town on the island for shopping, boasting market halls, shopping arcades and factory outlets.
The arcades extend along the Royal Road. The *Arcades Salaffa* consist of about three dozen shops (mainly boutiques) in the lower or middle price band. In the *Arcades*

*Continental* and *Arcades Currimjee (*called *Les Arcades* for short)*, you'll find off-the-peg designer clothing, young fashion, antiques and souvenirs. There's a small restaurant that offers snacks and coffee on the first floor of the Arcades Currimjee. *The shops are closed from 1pm on Thursdays. Wed and Sat are market days.*

### ANTIQUES

*L'Antiquaire* stocks small furniture, lamps and dishes. *Emile Sauzier Street | Mon–Wed and Fri/Sat 9.30am–5.30pm, Thu 9.30am–1pm*

### MADE IN CHINA

*Beautés de Chine* sells Chinese porcelain, carvings, table linen, jade, copper and small antiques. *Les Arcades | Route du Jardin | Mon–Wed and Fri 9.30am–5.30pm, Thu 9.30am–1pm*

### MARITIME

Ships trunks, travel desks, chests of drawers and beautiful model ships are sold in the *Galerie de la Marine | Royal Road | near the cathedral | Mon–Sat 9.30am–4.30pm*

### MODEL SHIPS

At the *Company Maquette José Ramar (Comajora* for short)*, the oldest and largest model ship factory on the island, you can watch the crafts people making maquettes. You can also buy and order models (from 8000 rupees). *At the southern end of town, turn right onto Brasserie Road | Forest Side (signposted) | Mon–Fri 9am–4pm, Sat 9am–1pm*

### JEWELLERY

You can buy duty-free jewellery, watches, and diamonds in the *Adamas* diamond factory. You can also look at jewellery being made in the workshop. *Mangal-khan Lane | Mon–Fri 9am–4pm, Sat 9am–noon*

### KNITWEAR

Cheap sweaters, polo shirts and T-shirts are sold in ★ *Floréal Square* on two floors. There are some branded goods and not all of the items are seconds by any means. *Mangalkhan Lane | close to the diamond factory | Mon–Fri 9.30am–5pm, Sat 9.30am–1pm*

## ENTERTAINMENT

### CASINO

Apart from roulette, there's also blackjack, restaurants, entertainment and dancing to be enjoyed. It's surprisingly elegant, but a collar and tie aren't compulsory. You can play on the one-armed

**MARCO POLO HIGHLIGHTS**

★ **Trou aux Cerfs**
Beautiful views from the edge of a volcano → p. 78

★ **Floréal Square**
Here you can purchase brand name clothes at cheap prices → p. 79

★ **Hotel Gool**
You can get nourishment for both body and soul from 'Gool' in Beau Bassin → p. 82

★ **Tamarin**
A picture perfect lagoon with palms and a beach, situated in front of the 'Matterhorn of Mauritius' → p. 83

★ **Casela Nature & Leisure Park**
Even the rare Mauritian falcon lives in this park: only the dodo's missing from the 140 species in this natural paradise near Tamarin → p. 84

bandits in the annexe from 10am, but you must wear long trousers and sleeves while you're there. *T. de Buch Street | Corner of Boulevard Victoria/Rue Thérèse | daily 9am–3am | tel. 6 02 13 00*

Life in the resort of Flic en Flac is as colourful as the houses

## WHERE TO STAY

### AUBERGE DE LA MADELON
A very simple but well-run property in the heart of Curepipe. *15 rooms | Pope Hennessy Street | tel. 6 70 18 85 | Budget*

### LE PLAZA HOTEL
This budget hotel in a central location is particularly popular with guests from La Réunion. *70 rooms | Impasse Pot de Terre | tel. 6 70 15 18 | plazahotelltd@intnet.mu | Budget*

## WHERE TO GO

### MARE AUX VACOAS (125 E2) (*ଫ C–D9*)
This is the largest lake and the most important reservoir on the island. It features
a hydroelectric power plant. It's named after the surrounding *vacoas* ('screw pines'). The prevailing temperature is cool because of its altitude (600m/1970ft). There's a beautiful round-trip walking trail. With hardwood and pine forest all around, the landscape looks more like Finland than the tropics. *7km/4mi to the south*

# FLIC EN FLAC & WOLMAR

**(120 A4–5) (*ଫ B8*) The 5km/3mi-long beach at Flic en Flac ranks among the most beautiful on the island. The waves of the Indian Ocean break on the reef around 100m from the shore.**

Because of the numerous, widely-scattered multi-storey buildings, Flic en Flac has become a bit of an urban sprawl, and the sugar cane fields have given way to holiday resorts. Most hotels are located on the southern stretch of beach by Wolmar. The only part of town with any atmosphere is the original district with its old fishing houses and small shops. If you want to experience Mauritius' cultural diversity, visit the nearby public beach. It's often very crowded, and particularly so at weekends and holidays. During these peak times, extended families come to sit around and have a picnic in the shade of the trees. Most of them also bring pre-cooked food with them in cooking pots. If you're not quite so well equipped, there are Chinese, Indian, Creole and Italian restaurants along the coastal road. They're mostly budget, but some are quite expensive, too.

## FOOD & DRINK

### SEA BREEZE
A restaurant that features Chinese and Creole cuisine; the fish dishes and sea-

food are highly recommended. *Wed–Mon | Royal Road | Flic en Flac | tel. 4 53 92 41 | Moderate*

## SHOPPING

### CASCAVELLE SHOPPING VILLAGE ●
This shopping centre is located on the left-hand side of the road that goes from Flic en Flac to Quatre Bornes. There are 60 shops, a supermarket and a large food court. You can reach the shopping centre from Flic en Flac by bus. You can also get here from Le Morne by public transport. *Mon–Thu 9.30am–8.30pm, Fri/Sat until 10pm, Sun until 3.30pm*

### PASADENA VILLAGE
There's a well-stocked supermarket in Pasadena Village, opposite the police station. On the building's first floor you'll find a pharmacy, a tourist information centre and lots of small souvenir and clothes shops. *Daily 10am–5.30pm (supermarket open until 8pm) | Royal Road | Flic en Flac*

## ENTERTAINMENT

### SHOTZ
Opposite the beach, young people come here to drink cocktails. Club Shotz comes alive with dancing to ambient and chart music. *No fixed opening times | Royal Road | Flic en Flac*

## WHERE TO STAY

### GOLD BEACH RESORT
A family-run hotel with a pool and a restaurant. *36 rooms | Wolmar | tel. 4 53 82 35 | www.goldbeachhotel.com | Moderate*

### HILTON MAURITIUS RESORT
A luxury hotel on the beach in Wolmar with three excellent restaurants, including the INSIDER TIP ▶ *Ginger Thai*. It also boasts great sports facilities and a spa. The complex also impresses visitors with its elaborate garden architecture and waterfalls. Rooms from 12,000 rupees. *193 rooms | Wolmar | tel. 4 03 10 00 | www.hilton.com | Expensive*

### JET-7
Several apartment complexes for self-caterers. Most come with a pool and are within walking distance of the beach at Flic en Flac. *Avenue Verger | tel. 4 53 96 00 | www.jet-7.com | Budget*

### THE NILAYA
A small complex with only four studios, located in a tropical garden with lots of shrubs and fruit trees, including mangos, bananas, papayas and lemons. Situated

## LOW BUDGET

▶ A local lunch: the *London Way* supermarket offers lunch, coffee and cake. The meals may be taken out or consumed on the terrace and cost around 110 rupees. Various Mauritian dishes are appetizingly presented in a glass case, so you can order easily without knowing the language. But fear not: the chilli comes separately! *Royal Road | Tamarin*

▶ The *Hotel Tamarin* offers dolphin tours by boat along the west coast. It's also open to non-residents. It costs 1000 rupees for a half-day tour without food. A tour including a picnic on Île aux Bénitiers will cost 1500 rupees. It's much cheaper than the normal full-day tours that include catering. *Mon–Sat 8am–11am | Booking ahead necessary | tel. 7 35 80 62*

not far from the beach and the lagoon. The owner Kit Graas will cook you a Mauritian evening meal on request. The price includes breakfast. *Avenue des Colombes | Flic en Flac | tel. 4 53 90 37 | www.nilaya-mauritius.com | Budget*

### LA PIROGUE HOTEL

This was one of the first hotels on the island, attracting a diverse crowd and offering vibrant entertainment. The complex includes round thatched bungalows that are modelled on traditional fishing boats and are located in the palm grove on the beach at Flic en Flac. There's a very extensive (water)sports programme. *248 rooms | Wolmar | tel. 4 53 84 41 | www.lapirogue.com | Expensive*

# QUATRE BORNES & BEAU BASSIN & ROSE HILL

**(120–121 C–D 3–4) (*m* C7–8) Due to the economic boom of recent years, Quatre Bornes (72,000 inhabitants) is called 'Millionaire City'**

Visitors mainly come here, however, because of the popular ● INSIDER TIP ▶ clothes market where you can buy individual items (knitwear, shirts, jeans, etc.) at particularly good prices.

*Beau Bassin* is the northernmost of the seven contiguous cities of the western highlands.

The transition from the Rose Hill business city is seamless. Life here revolves around the so-called plaza with its town hall, library and theatre. Situated in the adjacent local authority building, the *Galerie Max Boulle (Mon–Sat 10am–6pm)* occa-

sionally showcases the talent of Mauritian artists.

## FOOD & DRINK

### HAPPY RAJA

Exquisite Indian cuisine, situated on the main street near the police station. The restaurant is located in a small colonial house. There's a large selection of quality food at low prices. *Daily | Route St. Jean | Quatre Bornes | tel. 4 27 14 00 | Budget*

### HOTEL GOOL ★

An unusual snack bar that's open around the clock and provides a meeting point for night owls. It's popularly known to the locals as 'No Door', the owner originally wanting to save on the cost of having a night watchman. In the somewhat gloomy interior where everyone stands to eat, Indian music plays in the background and the racket of arcade games blares out from a side room. Gool, the owner, is Indian. He's an educated man and something of a philosopher, to whom stimulating conversation seems more important than selling snacks. *Daily | Road at the roundabout by the post office and the police station | Beau Bassin | Budget*

### KING DRAGON

Excellent Chinese restaurant with a café and the *Queen's Cabaret Club*. *Wed–Mon | Route St. Jean | Quatre Bornes | tel. 4 24 78 88 | Moderate*

## SHOPPING

The shopping opportunities in Rose Hill give Curepipe a run for its money. The most important shopping centres are the *Arcade Sunassee* on the *Royal Road, the Atrium Shopping Centre* on *Vandermeersch Street* and INSIDER TIP ▶ *Les*

Galeries Evershine in the Commercial Complex.

## ENTERTAINMENT

### INDIGO

This nightclub in the heart of Quatre Bornes is open on Fridays and Saturdays from 10pm until 5am. There's always something going on here. Route St. Jean | Entry 250 rupees

### THE LINK IN CYBERCITY

This bar in The Link Ebene City Hotel on the north-eastern edge of Quatre Bornes is open around the clock. On INSIDER TIP Friday afternoons, the rich young things of Mauritius meet here in the futuristic Cybercity with its call centres and internet firms to have a drink. Live music is played on the terrace every Friday evening. Daily | Ebene Cybercity 65 | Moderate

### QUEEN´S DISCO & NIGHT CLUB

This club is popular with a younger audience. You can dance into the early hours here on Friday and Saturday. Route St. Jean | Quatre Bornes | tel. 2 54 77 55 | Entry 200 rupees, 300 rupees on evenings with shows.

## WHERE TO STAY

### EL MONACO

A sprawling complex with a pool, it's very good value for money. 93 rooms | 17 Route St. Jean | Quatre Bornes | tel. 4 25 26 08 | www.el-monaco.com | Moderate

# TAMARIN

(120 A5) (ᗰ B8) ★ Most of the time the wide estuary of the Rivière Tamarin and the Rivière du Rempart is peaceful. Between July and September, however, surfers from all over the world flock here to experience the waves that slip through the gap in Mauritius' coral reef. The current conditions are posted on the internet (www.windguru.cz). Surfers from South Africa in particular fly here for a few days around this time. Inland from Tamarin, the 'Matterhorn of Mauritius' dominates the heights, the Montagne du Rempart (777 m/2550ft) being one of

The Montagne du Rempart near Tamarin is the 'Matterhorn of Mauritius'

the landmarks of the island. There are salt flats around this town, which experiences low levels of rainfall. The flats are increasingly giving way to settlements, but the salt is still piled up high.

## SIGHTSEEING

### CASELA NATURE & LEISURE PARK ★
(120 B4–5) (*∅ B8*)

Originally just a bird park, today the variety of animals here ranges from native monkeys and Javanese deer to zebras, kangaroos and wildcats. The focus, however, is still on the birds, of which there are now more than 1,500 specimens. You can see around 140 species here, including the extremely rare Mauritian pigeon and Mauritian kestrel. You can also arrange adventure tours in the wild landscape of the extensive grounds, including, for example, photo safaris in jeeps. Fearless visitors might also like to take a walk with lions and tigers: you can pet and stroke the big cats and even be photographed with them. The small walking tour is also great for the more adventurous, because you get to cross a 60m

deep gorge on a Nepalese suspension bridge and climb along a precipice, secured by a harness. Take your swimming costumes with you because you can swim in the small pool under one of the waterfalls. Lunch is also served here in the wild on a platform under the trees. There's a magnificent view from the 🌿 terrace of the *Casela Restaurant* (*Expensive*). *Daily 9am–6pm (May–Oct 9am–5pm) | Entry 325 rupees | Royal Road | Cascavelle | www.caselayemen.mu*

## SPORTS & ACTIVITIES

### SURFING

Surfboards and lessons are offered by Roger Theveneau *(1 hour including board hire for beginners is 700 rupees, 500 rupees for more advanced students)* at the Tamarin Hotel *(tel. 7 27 07 76)*. Also open to non-residents.

## WHERE TO STAY

### LEORA BEACH

An apartment complex situated right on the beach. The kitchen is fully equipped

Water sports fans are particularly attracted to the Bay of Tamarin in the summer months

and each apartment has a barbecue. Ideal for families and smaller groups. *12 apartments and 2 penthouses | tel. 4 52 10 10 | www.horizon.mu | Moderate*

### TAMARIN HOTEL

A simple but very charming hotel with a pool and a small spa. The bar and restaurant are also popular with the locals. *66 rooms | Tamarin Bay | tel. 4 83 69 27 | www.hoteltamarin.com | Budget–Moderate*

# VACOAS-PHOENIX

(121 D–E 4–5) *(ɯ D8)* **It's virtually impossible to define the boundaries of this city, so it's referred to as the double city of Vacoas-Phoenix. Around 92,000 people live here in total.**

Many textile factories produce their collections in this congested urban area. Thousands of people commute to work in the region. There are interesting shopping opportunities for visitors and you can also go dancing in the evenings with locals. Incidentally, one of Mauritius' three varieties of beer is also named after Phoenix. There's a market in Vacoas *Market (Sivananda Road)* on Tuesdays and Fridays, partly held in the new hall and partly in stalls outside.

### GLASS

The *Phoenix Glass Gallery* sells souvenirs made from recycled glass. Visitors can even watch the items being made. *Pont Fer | Phoenix | Mon–Sat 9am–11am and 1pm–3pm.*

### SHOPPING

You'll find shoe and clothes shops on many floors in the large *Phoenix Les Halles* shopping mall. There's also a supermarket and a food court and there are exhibitions by local artists from time to time. *Pont Fer | Phoenix | Mon–Thu 9.30am–8pm, Fri/Sat until 9pm, Sun until 2pm*

### TEXTILES

The *Ocean Factory Shop* specialises in leisure and swimwear fashion and always has good deals in its range. *Nalletamby Road 56 | Phoenix | Mon–Sat 8.30am–5.30pm*

### NEW SAVOY

A small cinema right in the centre of Vacoas with an Indian film programme. The Bollywood productions range from romantic love films to war dramas and there's nearly always singing and dancing. *Avenue Saint Paul/John Kennedy | Vacoas | Entry 200 rupees*

# TRIPS & TOURS

The tours are marked in green in the road atlas,
pull-out map and on the back cover

## 1 'MONDAY'S ROUTE': THE EASTERN PART OF THE ISLAND

Holidaymakers visit Mauritius because of the beaches and exclusive hotels. However, if you spend all your days by the sea, you'll miss out on an enchanting landscape. The small places in between the sugar cane fields or on the edge of the jungle also have their own charm. The nearly 80km/50mi car journey from Mahébourg to Poste de Flacq will familiarise you with this side of the island. The excursion lasts nearly a whole day.

You should do the tour through the east of Mauritius on a Monday. It's then that there's a market in Mahébourg → p. 62, the starting point of the route. This small

sleepy town is the only place of significant size in the southeast of the island. If you come from the west on the A10 to Mahébourg, the Tamil Temple of Shri Vinayaour Seedalamen → p. 63 will appear on the left-hand side; on the right-hand side there's also a small temple of prayer. Not far away is a colonial villa which housed the Naval Museum in 1950 and which has now been expanded into the National History Museum → p. 62. This magnificent building is apparently haunted; in any case, in the 19th century ghosts are supposed to have held fantastic balls here among the dilapidated furniture. The furniture has now given way to showcases and exhibits, but the house has nevertheless kept its ghostly atmosphere.

Photo: Waterfall in the Charamel Black River National Park

Discover the sleepy villages in the east of the island, or take a tour through the southwest and travel down from the highlands to the coast

The journey on the B28 leads north of Mahébourg. Sometimes close to the sea, sometimes in the foothills of the mountains, the route meanders through a sparsely inhabited region. Only now and then will you drive through villages. The small streets of these places are hardly surfaced, and the ramshackle wooden huts sometimes seem very poor. Despite this, the walls are often painted in all the colours of the rainbow. There are few attractions here, which is why an unassuming obelisk that commemorates the

landing of the first settlers on Mauritius is marked as a point of interest.

As you continue the landscape becomes more and more attractive. In the **Vallée de Ferney** Nature Reserve *(www.val leedeferney.com)*, the Mauritian Wildlife Foundation *(www.mauritian-wildlife.org)*, together with both the National Park and Conservation Service and the Forestry Service, are trying to restore the original forest and to reintroduce endangered bird species to an area of more than 220 hectares. You can get a good overview of the native flora and fauna during a 3km/2mi-long tour with a guide that lasts around 90 minutes.

**Vieux Grand Port → p. 66** was once, as the name suggests, the most important harbour on the island. Today, however, it's a bit of a nondescript dump. The protected old cemetery and the museum, which displays the history of the Dutch settlers, are certainly worth a visit. From then on the route follows the line of the coast. The 480m/1575ft-high **Montagne du Lion → p. 65** rises up on the left hand side, reminiscent of a reclining lion when seen from the south. Beyond Providence, a street sign in the bay of Anse Jonchée points the way to the **Kestrel Valley → p. 65** Nature Park, with its Ylang Ylang distillery. You can hunt, hike, and observe the wildlife here, but it's also a good stop for refreshments.

Before the street winds over the mountain down into Kestrel Valley, you'll pass a small administrative hut. You should enquire here about the condition of the road because the journey can become quite problematic, especially after heavy rainfall. Just under a quarter of an hour's drive will take you to ☀️ **INSIDER TIP** *Le Panoramour* restaurant *(daily 11am–3pm | reservation recommended | tel. 6 34 50 11 | Expensive)*. Here, in the foothills of the **Bambou Mountains**, you'll feel as if you've been transported to an oasis of calm. Only the chirping of birds and the screech of monkeys can be heard. There are also Javanese deer in the forests, introduced by the Dutch from Indonesia, and wild pigs. Many visitors come here to observe the wildlife, and others come to hunt: a trophy is (almost) guaranteed. As a result, the restaurant serves, among other things, fresh wild game.

If you're in the mood for seafood at lunchtime, content yourself with a drink

The décor of this Kestrel Valley restaurant doesn't leave any doubt: fresh game is definitely on the menu

at the bar and be patient until you get to Bambous Virieux. A short drive further north on the B28 will take you to the stone houses of the unconventional Le Barachois → p. 64 hotel (16 bungalows | tel. 6 34 56 43 | www.lebarachois.com | Expensive), which are located in shallow water on the Pointe Bambou. It's surrounded by an oyster farm and boasts an excellent cuisine. Leave the B28 in the small town of Bel Air → p. 62, above which rises the double tower of the Saint Esprit church. Then take the B55 West towards Camp de Masque.

On the way you'll get to see nature's more lavish side. Hibiscus bushes, banana plants, palms, and thousands of wild flowers grow from the valleys right up into the heights of Montagne Fayence and Montagne Blanche.

From Unité take the A7 to Centre de Flacq → p. 61. This town is located on the great plains and nestles between sugar cane plantations. The region around Flacq was one of the most densely settled and productive areas on Mauritius during the time of French rule. Indeed, the island's largest sugar refinery stood here at the start of the 19th century. Today Flacq has become a lonely place, only really coming to life now on market days.

From Centre de Flacq, follow the B23 to Poste de Flacq → p. 61 where a Hindu Temple stands on a headland. On the other side of the bay you can make out the outlines of the Saint Géran Hotel. In order to get there, follow the B62 south and past the new golf course at the Belle Mare Plage → p. 60 hotel. At the fork in the road, turn left to Le Saint Géran → p. 60, one of the most beautiful hotels on the island. Here you can end your day in perfect style with a cool cocktail or with a visit to try your luck in the hotel's casino.

## 2 THE SOUTH WEST PASSAGE: A TOUR THROUGH EVERY CLIMATE

Large parts of the south of the island still give the impression of what Mauritius must have looked like before settlers arrived here. The route is around 60km/40mi long and takes one day to complete.

Before you start, you should stock up with at least some drinks and a couple of snacks for the journey.

The tour begins at Curepipe → p. 76. This place was founded after the malaria epidemic of 1866. From its location 550m/1800ft above sea level, the city's founders thought it promised a better climate than the one they'd experienced next to the sea, apparently ignoring the fact that this is the wettest spot on the whole island. Rain showers fall here every day.

The journey begins directly beyond Floréal → p. 76, Curepipe's neighbouring town. From here on you can immerse yourself in the solitude of the highlands. At the point at which the B3 and the B70 meet, follow the small country lane to the south in the direction of Le Pétrin. The landscape is hilly and pine forests stretch in every direction. Fog often hangs over the trees and the area almost gives the impression of being Nordic. After around 10km/6mi you'll reach the Mare aux Vacoas → p. 80, the largest freshwater lake on the island. It's used both as a drinking water reservoir and for the operation of a hydroelectric plant, but a dam blocks the view of the lake. At regular intervals, however, there are steps that you can take to reach the top of the dam. You are almost 600m/1950ft above sea level here, and yet the road continues to climb.

Colourful statues at Grand Bassin, the Hindu's sacred lake

Le Pétrin → p. 70 hardly earns the title of village at all and consists of just a few small houses. Therefore, make sure you don't miss the big sign pointing to the Shivaratree Temple complex at Grand Bassin → p. 70, the holy lake of the Hindus. There are small shrines situated all along this ruler-straight road. Even more surprising is the sight from the pilgrims' car park of the large wind power turbine. It's evidence of Mauritius' use of the south-easterly trade winds as an energy source.

Hindus expect to get a completely different type of energy from a visit to Grand Bassin, however. Even just the large car park, with space for hundreds of cars, makes it clear how important the place is to them. The mighty statue of Shiva at the far end also consolidates the impression. Almost as tall as the Statue of Liberty in New York's harbour, the deity welcomes believers with a wave of his hand and a smile on his lips. Like a lighthouse, the figure rises out of the landscape and shows the way to the shrine. According to legend, Shiva took a world tour in a flying ship with his wife Parvati, during which he wanted to show her the most beautiful places on earth. Mauritius was one of the stops on his route where he's said to have spilled a little of the amphora of water that he'd taken from the River Ganges and that was balanced on his head. The drops fell down into the crater of Grand Bassin and, as belief would have it, this is how the lake was created.

During the Maha Shivaratree celebrations in February/March, the largest Hindu festival outside India, hundreds of thousands of white-clad believers gather here. Dancing, praying and singing, they step into the lake and sprinkle offerings of flowers. During the rest of the year, however, it's peaceful at Grand Bassin. Half-tame monkeys jump all around and show little respect for any offerings. In good weather it's worth climbing up the steps to the 700m/2300ft-high summit of Piton Grand Bassin.

Now drive back to Le Pétrin on the main road and turn left towards the south. Travelling across the plateau of Plaine

Champagne → p. 70, you'll reach the Macchabée nature reserve, the roof of Mauritius. For this part of the journey the landscape is barren, rough, and at times seems ugly and anything but tropical. Along the 20km/12mi stretch to Chamarel, however, the picture changes dramatically. The bumpy road takes countless curves and small paths lead off again and again into the hidden corners of the highlands. Signs reading 'View Point' point to good spots to take in the area's natural beauty, including one that overlooks the 🔆 Alexandra Falls. The route then travels through the dense undergrowth of the forest and emerges at steep cliffs and spectacular gorges: images of a primeval jungle landscape.

Probably the most beautiful viewing point is at 🔆 Black River Gorges, around 8 km/5mi from Le Pétrin. 200m beyond the car park, the view opens up to look over a mighty waterfall. The gorge, eaten into the mountain by the river, continues down to the ocean. When visibility is good you can make out the Tamarin plain as well as the Black River Peak, the highest mountain on the island at 828m/2717ft. A poorly signposted hiking trail begins a few hundred feet further south down the road; the hike lasts approx. three hours. Continuing the journey, a very worthwhile break can be had in the Varangue sur Morne → p. 70 restaurant (daily 11.30am–3.30pm | tel. 4 83 57 10 | Moderate–Expensive) where there's a veranda situated above banana and pineapple plantations. For lunch you should make a stop at the entrance to Chamarel → p. 69 at the 🙂 L'Alchimiste restaurant (Mon–Sat | tel. 4 83 79 80 | Moderate) where they serve organic food.

From here drive south and follow the signs to Terres des Sept Couleurs → p. 70. The drive now starts to lead through sugar cane fields. The first attraction on this private road is on the left: the 90m/300ft-high Cascade Chamarel waterfall. The goal, however, is to reach the rare geological phenomenon of the 'coloured earth'. A row of bare hills undulates gently through the lush, tropical vegetation. At first glance the ground looks rust red, but it actually shimmers with oxidised volcanic lava rock in seven colours. Back on the main road, the 🔆 route descends south to Baie du Cap. Since the road here has finally been developed and freshly surfaced, the driver can also enjoy the magnificent view. An equally beautiful 🔆 alternative route travels back to Chamarel and then down the

The Macaque monkey also sometimes appreciates a snack

west coast to Case Noyale. On both routes, you quickly leave the plateau and travel towards the coast on narrow, winding roads. The view is often magnificent, the sparkling sea stretching right out to the horizon beyond. As you drive, the temperature rises every second you descend. As a result, the anticipation of a cool drink and a swim in the ocean becomes ever more enticing.

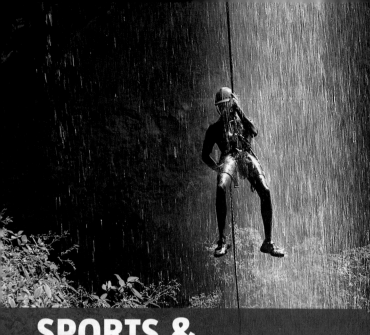

# SPORTS & ACTIVITIES

**The Mauritian's fondness for cricket and horse racing is very British. Football and athletics are also very popular with the locals.**

Holidaymakers have a wide range of sporting activities to choose from. The calm lagoons with their gentle currents offer great conditions for water sports, and wave riders will definitely get their money's worth at Tamarin.

The sports offered by the hotels are tailored to beginners and experts alike – hardly a wish is left unfulfilled. The hotels' wellness centres (spas) and massage salons will take care of all your relaxation needs.

## CYCLING TOURS

All hotels rent bikes. The low-traffic stretches along the east coast are particularly suitable for cycling tours. Great routes can be found on the Blue Bay peninsula in the southeast, at Morne Brabant, and on the northern tip of the island at Cap Malheureux. Mountain bikers can find more demanding routes in the mountains of Kestrel Valley and in the Black River Gorges National Park.

## DEEP SEA FISHING

Mauritius is considered a paradise for serious anglers. Various organisations offer professionally equipped boats with experienced crews. For a six-hour fishing trip on the Indian Ocean, you'll pay in the region of 2000 rupees; the yachts rarely come back without a catch. The high sea-

**Golf, hiking, surfing and sailing: whether on dry land or in the water, if there's an activity you want to do, they'll have it on Mauritius**

son for the coveted blue marlin is November to April; sharks, bonitos, barracuda, and tuna bite all year round. Booking and information at: *La Carangue | Rivière Noire | tel. 7299497; La Misaine | Trou aux Biches | tel. 2655209; Sportfisher | Grand Baie | tel. 2638358.* The 'Marlin Masters' angling competition takes place off the coast of Morne Brabant in February. This international competition is primarily aimed at professional anglers who come here from all over the world. *www.blackriver-mauritius.com*

## DIVING

Over 50 interesting diving spots of varying degrees of difficulty can be reached by boat in just a short time. The diving schools (for example in Trou aux Biches and Cap Malheureux) offer courses at all levels. Experienced divers should bring their certification, their logbook and a medical certificate proving that they are fit to dive. The association of Mauritian amateur divers, the *Mauritian Underwater Group,* meets socially every Tuesday at 7.30pm. *MUG | Railway Road | Phoenix | tel. 6 96 53 68 | www.mug.mu*

## EXTREME SPORTS

Vertical World offers canyoning and rock climbing *(tel. 6 97 54 30 | www.vertical worldltd.com)* and *Skydive Austral Mauritius* organises tandem parachute jumps. *Skydive Austral Mauritius (tel. 4 21 49 87 | www.skydivemauritius.com).*

If you'd rather have a more gradual introduction to extreme sports, the zip line tours at Soft Adventure are the thing for you. Near St Félix there are various lengths of steel cable that span the width of the Rivière des Galets. Hooked on to them with a harness and attached to a roller, you'll zip along and almost believe you're flying over the valley. Together with the walk back through the forest and a bathing stop under a waterfall, the trip takes five hours. *Cost: 2200 rupees | www.incentivepartnersltd.com*

Long distance runners train in the canyons of the Black River and on the slopes of Le Pouce on most Saturdays from November. They're preparing for the *Royal Raid*. These 80km/50mi and 35km/22mi cross-country races take place each year in April or May. Participants come from as far as Europe, Africa and Australia. Information: *tel. 6 22 21 48* or *6 22 72 34*, on the Internet: *www.royalraid.com*

## GOLF

Several hotels on Mauritius have wonderful golf courses, sometimes located directly by the sea. Green fees are sometimes included in the price of your stay. The 18-hole championship course (par 71) at Belle Mare Plage ranks among the best. Another notable 18-hole golf course on the east coast can be found on Mauritius' offshore Île aux Cerfs *(www.ileaux cerfsgolf.com)*. The 18-hole course (par 72) of Le Paradis and Dinarobin hotels at Morne Brabant is sophisticated and has a superb location. The west coast has a

The sails are stowed away and the sun begins its slow descent

further public course in Tamarina (18 hole, par 72). In the newly developed southern region, the Bel Ombre Golf course (18 holes, par 72) has emerged as an impressive facility. Golfers can also become temporary members of the *Gymkhana Club* (18 holes, par 68) in Vacoas *(Green fee 1600 rupees | Plaine Williams)*.

## HORSERIDING

You can experience the beaches of Belle Mare, Trou aux Biches and Flic en Flac on horseback. Many hotels organise horse rides *(Prices approx. 1000 rupees for 30 min)*. Carriage rides are also offered by the Coco Beach, Sugar Beach, La Pirogue and Domaine Les Pailles hotels. Experienced riders will find just what they need at *Haras du Morne (tel. 7 05 16 44 | from approx. 3500 rupees)*.

## HIKING

The mountain kingdoms of the east and the south are particularly good for hiking. Beautiful 90-minute tours head off from the *Montagne du Lion* (480 m/1575ft) at Vieux Grand Port, and longer two to three-hour tours go to the peak of *Le Pouce* (812 m/2664ft) at Port Louis. Climbing fans can climb the *Pieter Both* (823 m/2700ft) with *Vertical World (tel. 6 97 54 30)*. Guided walks are offered in the east by *Kestrel Valley (tel. 6 34 50 11)*, in the west by *Yanature (tel. 7 85 6177)* and in the south by *Domaine Chazal (tel. 4 22 3117)*.

## SAILING

From June to September a stiff breeze blows in, especially on the east coast. The hotels have the necessary equipment ready and they'll help you out, and you can also have private lessons. Catamaran tours are available at *Croisières Australes and Harris Wilson (north west coast) | tel. 6 76 36 95 and at Croisières Turquoises (East and South Coast) | tel. 6 31 83 47.* The hotels and *Yacht Charter Ltd. | Grand Baie | tel. 2 63 83 95* will provide information about chartering yachts.

## WALKING UNDERWATER

Walking across the bottom of the sea in an air-filled glass box is a fantastic experience that won't even mess up your hair. These extraordinary underwater walks are offered at *Belle Mare*, *Cap Malheureux,* in *Blue Bay*, and in the North *(approx. 1300 rupees for 30 min)*. Bookings can be made with: *Underseawalk Discovery | tel. 7 28 35 75; and Solar Sea Walk | tel. 2 63 78 19*

## WINDSURFING

The lagoon is an ideal spot for windsurfing and kitesurfing. Almost all of the hotels provide boards for free, and courses are also available. Experts love the challenging seas off the **INSIDER TIP** southern tip of the Morne Brabant peninsula from June to October. In the middle of August, the kitesurfing event Kiteival takes place in several locations throughout the island, providing plenty of exciting events for spectators *(www.kiteivalmauritius.com)*. Moreover, Mauritius also plays host to the Kite Surf Pro Wave Tour *(www.kspworldtour.com)*. Stand up paddle surfing – using a paddle to propel a surfboard through the water like a boat – has enjoyed great popularity in recent times. Schools can be found at Cap Malheureux *(www.sindbad.mu | tel. 2 62 88 36)*, in Le Morne *(www.club-mistral.com | tel. 4 50 41 12)* and at Belle Mar-Palmar *(www.mauritius-kitesurf.com | tel. 7 43 42 98)*.

# TRAVEL
# WITH KIDS

**Children are very welcome as guests on Mauritius. This is certainly due in part to the fact that families with six or more offspring are far from uncommon on the island.**

Children can play without a care in the water of the shallow, warm lagoons that are free from dangerous currents and waves. With a pinch of imagination, they can build castles and mountains out of sand, seashells and pieces of coral. Especially at Christmas, Easter and in July/August, kids have a lot of playmates of their own age in the hotel complexes, and there's a great deal of variety for them to get stuck into.

You should definitely pack swimming things, waterproof sun cream and a sun hat. It's also very useful to bring bathing shoes for protection against sea urchins and sharp pieces of coral.

The beach hotels are generally very family-friendly. If you're travelling to Mauritius with your family, you should ensure when booking that your chosen accommodation is geared towards children. It's important to have a shallow pool and an extensive leisure programme. Discounts for children vary depending on the season. Many resorts also include Kids' Clubs which are excellently equipped and come complete with well-run childcare centres in which professional teams will care for guests aged from three to twelve. They offer sports classes, theatre performances, costume parties, adventure games, and even movies and special menus on their programmes that run

**Fun in the water and tropical life: on Mauritius, kids can splash around in the sea and enjoy exploring a foreign culture**

from morning 'til late afternoon and most activities take place in English or French.

Some hotels, including La Pirogue, Sugar Beach and Touessrok, offer special additional facilities and a leisure programme for young people. The staff at INSIDER TIP @sungeneration.com-Clubs make sure that young people will never get bored. Their programme includes activities ranging from day trips to disco evenings. Beyond that, there are also computers with internet access and a large selection of games is available. All clubs for children are free.

The Mauritian people are exceptionally child-friendly. If you're with your children in restaurants or out shopping, people will immediately come up to you and start chatting with your little ones. You won't have any problem at all finding jars of baby food or nappies/diapers in all the standard sizes in the island's supermarkets.

## THE NORTH

### THE BOTANICAL GARDEN
(118 B5) (*⑽ E5*)

A popular destination for trips in the small town of Pamplemousses with more than 80 types of palms, giant lily pads and spice trees. The local guides explain everything very vividly. *Daily 8am–5pm | Entry 100 rupees, guided tour 75 rupees per person*

### PÉREYBÈRE (118 C2) (*⑽ E3*)

Children can have a great time splashing around with many local families on the protected beach at this popular bathing spot. Péreybère is located in the shadow of the hustle and bustle of Grand Baie. The town's restaurants, shops and cafés can be reached in just a few minutes.

### UNDERWATER TOURS (118 B3) (*⑽ D3*)

You can dive down in a real submarine to get fascinating insights into life under water (*Blue Safari | Trou aux Biches | at the Coralia Mont Choisy Hotel | tel. 2 63 33 33 | Journey approx. 3900 rupees, children 2300 rupees*). A ride on an underwater scooter is also a unique experience (*also Blue Safari | 5000 rupees for two people per vehicle, 3900 rupees for one person*).

## PORT LOUIS

### DOMAINE LES PAILLES
(121 D2) (*⑽ D6*)

Children can take a ride on the reproduction railway here or travel in a historic horse and carriage. In the sugar mill (an authentic replica of the original) you can learn how sugar cane becomes sugar and rum. *Prices vary depending on what you'd like to do | www.domainelespailles. net*

### HARBOUR TOUR (U A2) (*⑽ a2*)

Tours set off every day from Caudan Waterfront, the shopping and entertainment complex (*daily 10am–6.30pm | trip costs approx. 250 rupees*, family discounts available*). The tours give an insight into the hustle and bustle of this enormous merchandise trading point.

## THE EAST

### KESTREL VALLEY (127 E1) (*⑽ G9*)

A visit to this hunting property is always very diverse. You'll be able to take a walk and discover deer and wild boar in the middle of this unspoilt forest. With a bit of luck you'll also be able to observe the extremely rare Mauritian kestrel in the wild. Prices vary depending on the what you'd like to do | *tel. 6 34 50 97 | www. kestrelvalley.com*

### INSIDER TIP ▶ LE WATERPARK & LEISURE VILLAGE (123 E3) (*⑽ G–H6*)

If you've not yet had enough fun in the sea, you'll get your money's worth at this waterpark. The little ones can really let off steam in the wave pool or in the children's pool with mini slides. Towels are not supplied. *In summer: daily 10am–6pm, in winter until 5.30pm | Entry 350 rupees, children 185 rupees | Belle Mare | www.lewaterpark.intnet.mu*

## THE SOUTH WEST

### CHAZAL (125 D5) (*⑽ C11*)

In this private area at St Félix, children from four years of age can glide on high wires over ravines and rivers, all in complete security. There are also small walking tours that lead past sugar canes and banana plants. An unforgettable experience for the whole family. *Incentive Partners | 2300 rupees, children 1600 rupees including food | tel. 4 22 31 17*

**DOLPHIN TOURS** (124 B–C2) (*ɰ B9*)
Dolphins live in the bay off Tamarin. The best chance to spot them is to get up early in the morning and observe them from a boat. With a little bit of luck you can also swim with the animals. A maximum of twelve people is taken on each trip. Professional staff ensure that the animals don't become stressed and provide guests with comprehensive informa-

*150 rupees, Sat/Sun 185 rupees, children 80 rupees | Senneville | Rivière des Anguilles*

## THE WEST

**CASELA NATURE & LEISURE PARK** (120 B4–5) (*ɰ B8*)
Every child will marvel at the great variety of birds you can see here: owls look

On Mauritius children have their every need taken care of

tion about these marine mammals' living habits. The trip lasts about two hours. The meeting point is the Island Sports Club in Grande Rivière Noire. *1200 rupees, children 800 rupees | Dolswim | tel. 4 22 92 81 | www.dolswim.com*

**INSIDER TIP LA VANILLE RÉSERVE DES MASCAREIGNES** (126 A5) (*ɰ D11*)
Crocodiles, monkeys and giant tortoises live in this park. Whether or not you'll let your children loose feeding the crocodiles (11am) is up to you. *Daily 9.30am–5pm | Entry Mon–Fri 270 rupees, children*

at you with a fixed gaze and parrots flutter through the enclosures. Do you know the difference between lemurs and monkeys, or between kangaroos and wallabies? If not, you'll find the answer here! It's also possible to play minigolf, fish or take a mini safari for an extra charge (approx. 80 rupees). There's also a petting zoo where children can feed the animals. You can also take part in a fishing contest and have fun on a bouncy castle. *May–Oct daily 9am–5pm, Nov–April 9am–6 pm | Adults 325, children 200 rupees | Royal Road | Cascavelle*

# FESTIVALS & EVENTS

Mauritius is a melting pot of cultures and religions. The various influences introduced by the Mauritian populations of Hindus, Christians, Buddhists, Muslims and Taoists are evident in their wide variety of celebrations and there's a large number of public holidays throughout the year. Due to the wide range of religious groups, very few festival days fall on constant dates, and instead 'wander' to some extent throughout the year. Therefore, it's a good idea to find out when they'll be celebrated for when you're travelling.

## FIXED PUBLIC HOLIDAYS

**1 and 2 Jan** *New Year*; **1 Feb** *Day of the Liberation of Slaves*; **12 Mar** *Independance Day and Republic Day*; **1 May** *Labour Day*; **9 Sept** *Père Laval Day*; **1 Nov** *All Saints' Day*; **2 Nov** *Memorial Day for the first Indian immigrants (1835)*; **25 Dec** *Christmas*

## CHANGING PUBLIC HOLIDAYS & CELEBRATIONS

### JANUARY/FEBRUARY

▶ The first few days in the New Year are marked by ● family gatherings. In small villages holidaymakers are sometimes invited in from the street.

▶ ★ *Cavadee:* This Hindu festival is the most spectacular on the island. After many weeks of fasting and meditation comes the day of the procession when the Tamil population stick needles through their faces, tongues, chests and backs. With great effort, they wear the colourfully decorated cavadee. Milk urns dangle on two sides of an arch from which nothing is spilled or allowed to run.

▶ *Chinese New Year:* Chinese families decorate the whole house with the lucky colour red. Offerings are given in the pagodas. Parades are held in the street and fireworks crackle everywhere you go.

### FEBRUARY

▶ *Id-al-Ada:* Muslims commemorate Abraham who was ready to sacrifice his son. After prayers in the Mosque a lamb is symbolically sacrificed.

### FEBRUARY/MARCH

▶ *Maha Shivaratree:* During this celebration, the largest Hindu festival outside India, around 300,000 Hindus dressed in white go down to the holy volcanic lake of Grand Bassin in order to honour the god Shiva. There they en-

## From the Hindu Festival of Light to the Chinese New Year: Mauritian celebrations traverse cultures and religions

gage in ritual washing and make sacrifices.

### MARCH

▶ *Holi:* This Hindu festival two weeks before the Indian New Year concerns the legend of Prince Pralad who celebrated when his evil aunt Holika died in a fire. The people throw straw effigies onto funeral pyres and splash each other with paint.

### MARCH/APRIL

▶ *Ugadi:* A New Year's festival held by the descendants of the people from the Indian region of Andhra Pradesh. It's the beginning of a new lunar calendar with prayers being said and resolutions made.

### AUGUST/SEPTEMBER

▶ *Ganesh Chaturthi:* This Indian festival is held in honour of Ganesh, the elephant-headed god.

### SEPTEMBER

▶ ★ *Père Laval Day:* On 9 September, locals of all faiths make a pilgrimage to the Church of Sainte Croix, the tomb of the national saint who selflessly cared for the poor and the slaves.

### OCTOBER/NOVEMBER

▶ INSIDER TIP *Divali:* This happiest of all Hindu festivals symbolises the victory of good over evil. Houses are lavishly decorated with candles, oil lamps and, today, electric fairy lights.

### NOVEMBER/DECEMBER

▶ *Ganga Asnan:* A Hindu festival held on the seashore. As the Ganges flows into the Indian Ocean, bathing in the sea gives celebrants purity and new strength.

▶ *Teemeedee:* A Tamil festival that's celebrated on the island throughout the year, but mainly from November to February. The highlight is when celebrants run over glowing coals.

# LINKS, BLOGS, APPS & MORE

LINKS

▶ www.mauritian-wildlife.org – This website tells you all about the work of the Mauritian Wildlife Foundation, a group of conservationists who are trying to reintroduce the original flora and fauna of the island. There's even a game that teaches you to recognise eight types of endangered Mauritian lizard.

▶ www.expatmauritius.com Love the island so much that you don't want to leave? This extensive website will tell you all the details you need to know about upping sticks and starting a new life in this tropical paradise.

▶ www.bbc.co.uk/languages/french You can get by with English on the island, but why not brush up on your French before you go? This website is full of excellent resources, including key words and phrases to help you communicate with the locals.

BLOGS & FORUMS

▶ www.weluvmu.wordpress.com The blog of an NGO that campaigns for the environment and social welfare on Mauritius. Great for finding out about the efforts to preserve the island's natural beauty. The main website is at www.welovemauritius.org

▶ http://www.yashvinblogs.com/ A great blog written by a Mauritian named Yashvin. This excellent site features regular posts about aspects of everyday life on the island. It's geared toward Mauritians, so it displays a side of life you might not otherwise experience. Includes some great photos.

▶ www.mauritiusphotography.com A team of photographers goes round and photographs the most beautiful spots on the island, and then uploads their snaps onto this website. The photographs are arranged by region. It's good preparation for your trip and excellent for reminiscing.

Regardless of whether you are still preparing your trip or already in Mauritius: these addresses will provide you with more information, videos and networks to make your holiday even more enjoyable

▶ http://www.radiomoris.com/ A radio station you can listen to online. There's also a wealth of audio samples that will get you tapping you feet and help you get to grips with the island's music scene.

▶ www.dodosite.com A site dedicated to this most famous of flightless birds. It's written by a British enthusiast who currently calls the island his home. He's even written several books on the subject.

VIDEOS, STREAMS & PODCASTS

▶ http://ile-maurice.tripod.com 'Life's too short to eat bad foods' – so goes the motto of this site, a wonderful collection of recipes telling you how to recreate the delicacies you've enjoyed on your trip. The sizzling sound that greets you when you open the site will get your taste buds tingling.

▶ www.mauritiusturfclub.com Want to get in the mood for the horse races at the Champ de Mars? This vibrant website has frequent updates about one of the island's favourite obsessions.

▶ The Big Guide of Mauritius Island (iOS): If a picture says more than a thousand words, what does a video say? In this app you'll find 15 videos about the most important attractions and the most significant religious festivals on the island.

▶ Online Radio Mauritius (iOS): Do you want to listen to Indian hits, Chinese Folklore, French classics, English pop and sega and 'seggae'? This app lets you access the radio stations on Mauritius so that you can check out all the latest tunes.

▶ Mauritius Offline Map Travel Guide (iOS)/Mauritius Offline Mappa Map (Android): These apps let you take detailed maps of the island with you wherever you go. You don't even need to be connected to the internet. You can also go online and pinpoint your position if you get lost in the sugar cane fields ...

APPS

▶ www.winmauritius.net WIN (Women In Networking) is an organisation that campaigns for women's rights on the island. Their website includes such campaigns as 'Men against Violence'.

NETWORKS

# TRAVEL TIPS

## ARRIVAL

✈ Air Mauritius (www.airmauritius.com) and British Airways (www.britishairways.com) fly direct to Mauritius from London in 12–13 hours. Flights with transfers are offered by Air France, KLM and Emirates, among others. A flight costs from approx. 420 £/670 $, and package deals are often worthwhile. The international airport is located in Mahébourg. There are no direct flights from the USA. Emirates, KLM and British Airways offer flights with transfers from around 940 £/1500 $. Flights from New York take around 21 hours. There aren't any direct flights from Canada either and flights from Toronto often stop in New York or Paris (or both). Such flights cost approx. 940 £/1500 $ and take around 23 hours.

## BEACH SELLERS

Wherever there are tourists, there are beach sellers too. Always assume that the prices are inflated. What are sold as 'local craft products' are often cheap imported goods. Have a look in the stores first to get a rough idea of the prices. Then you'll be much better placed to negotiate prices with the beach sellers.

## BOAT RENTALS

On Mauritius motorboats can only be rented with a skipper; you can't explore the ocean on your own. Small sailing boats and kayaks can be rented in hotels and you're allowed to go it alone within the boundary of the reef.

## BUSES

Public buses run to almost every village. It's the cheapest way to travel, and gives an insight into the lives of the locals. Each town has a central bus station. In urban areas buses operate from 5.30am to 8pm and from 6.30am to 6.30pm in the countryside. Tickets are only available from the conductors.

## CAR HIRE

Cars can be rented from 2000 rupees per day (excluding 15 per cent tax and insurance fees). The minimum age at which you can rent is 21 years. It's advisable to book in advance in December and January.

## CARS

They drive on the left in Mauritius. On roundabouts the person on the right has the right of way. The speed limit is 50km/30mi per hour in villages, otherwise it's 80 km/50 mi per hour and

## RESPONSIBLE TRAVEL

It doesn't take a lot to be environmentally friendly whilst travelling. Don't just think about your carbon footprint whilst flying to and from your holiday destination but also about how you can protect nature and culture abroad. As a tourist it is especially important to respect nature, look out for local products, cycle instead of driving, save water and much more. If you would like to find out more about eco-tourism please visit: www.ecotourism.org

# From arrival to weather

**From the start to the end of the holiday:
useful addresses and information for your trip to Mauritius**

110km/68mi per hour on the motorway. The motorway between the airport in the south and Grande Baie in the north is well developed. The rest of the approximately 1600km/1000mi-long road network consists mainly of narrow, winding rural roads.

## CONSULATES & EMBASSIES

### BRITISH HONORARY CONSULATE
*7th Floor, Les Cascades Building | Edith Cavell Street | Port Louis | tel. 230 202 94 00*

### US EMBASSY
*4th Floor, Rogers House | John Kennedy Avenue | PO Box 544 | Port Louis | tel. 230 202 40 00 | usembass@intnet.mu*

### THE CONSULATE OF CANADA
*18 Jules Koenig Street | Port Louis | tel. 230 212 5500 | canada@intnet.mu*

## CLIMATE

The peak season is between November and April. Even then, although it's the rainy season, the rainfall rarely lasts long. The humidity is around 90 per cent. Temperatures in the day are an average of 30°C/86°F. The water temperature can reach approximately 27°C/80°F. On the sheltered west coast the average air temperature is around 3–4°C/5–7°F higher. It's 5°C/9°F lower in the central highlands. In the Mauritian winter (May to October), it's around 7°C/12°F colder than in summer.

## CRIME

Mauritius is a safe holiday destination. Nevertheless, tourists are recommended to avoid deserted beaches and poorer residential areas, especially after dark, as criminal assaults can occur. Be aware of pickpockets, especially in crowded areas. If you change large sums of money, you should take care when leaving the bank.

## BUDGETING

| | |
|---|---|
| Snacks | Approx. 0.20 £/0.30 $ *for three samosas on the street* |
| Coffee | Approx. 2.00 £/3.00 $ *for a cup in a hotel* |
| Wine | Approx. 3.20 £/5.00 $ *for a ¼ litre carafe (approx. 8.5oz)* |
| Pineapples | Approx. 0.80 £/1.30 $ *each on the market* |
| Fuel | Approx. 0.80 £/1.30 $ *for 1 litre (approx. ¼ gallon) of unleaded gasoline* |
| Taxi | 8.00 £/13.00 $ *per hour* |

## CUSTOMS

Visitors aged 16 and over have a duty-free import allowance of: 200 cigarettes, 50 cigars or 250g of tobacco; 1l/33.8oz of spirits and 2l/67.6oz of wine or beer; and 25ml/0.84oz of eau de toilette. Importing weapons, drugs, pornographic material, cigarette papers, fruit, vegetables, meat and plants is forbidden.

## ELECTRICITY

220/230 V AC, British plugs. Adapters can be bought on the island or in hotels.

Police: *tel. 999*, Ambulance service: *tel. 114*, Fire service: *tel. 995*

## HEALTH

There aren't any epidemic tropical diseases on Mauritius and you mustn't fear poisonous animals either. The island is practically malaria-free. A high level of sun protection is essential. Tap/faucet water should not be drunk. Taking mosquito repellent is advisable. Because of sea urchins and sharp coral in shallow water, you should wear bathing shoes. Even small wounds should be disinfected right away. Sea urchin stings should be removed by a doctor. Digestive problems can be helped with a spoonful of black papaya seeds.

Most hotels work with contracted doctors. Travel health insurance is recommended. The selection of medications carried by the pharmacies meets European and American standards. Should you need to go to a hospital, you have a choice between government-run facilities, which also treat tourists for free, and private clinics where you have to pay in cash. In the case of severe illness, the private clinics are definitely recommended. There's a ban on importing some medications. Make sure to take a doctor's prescription with you and keep your medication in its original packaging. You can ask for a list of banned pharmaceutical products in the Mauritian embassy in your home country.

### CLINICS

*Clinique Darné | Rue Georges Gilbert | Floréal | tel. 6012300 | www.cliniquedarne. com; Clinique du Nord | Royal Road | Baie du Tombeau | tel. 2472532 | www.clini quedunord.com*

## IMMIGRATION

EU citizens, Americans, Australians, Canadians and New Zealanders need a passport valid for at least six months for a stay of up to three months on the island. Children need their own passport (a photo is required from the age of six). Anyone travelling from areas affected with cholera or yellow fever must submit proof of vaccination. An entry visa can only be obtained at the airport if you can show that you have a ticket for a flight out and a hotel reservation (or a booking for another form of accommodation).

# CURRENCY CONVERTER

| £ | MUR | MUR | £ |
|---|---|---|---|
| 1 | 50 | 1 | 0.02 |
| 2 | 100 | 20 | 0.40 |
| 5 | 250 | 50 | 1 |
| 7 | 350 | 100 | 2 |
| 15 | 750 | 250 | 5 |
| 25 | 1,250 | 750 | 15 |
| 30 | 1,500 | 1,500 | 30 |
| 50 | 2,500 | 4,000 | 80 |
| 100 | 5,000 | 10,000 | 200 |

| $ | MUR | MUR | $ |
|---|---|---|---|
| 1 | 31.50 | 1 | 0.03 |
| 2 | 63 | 20 | 0.63 |
| 5 | 158 | 50 | 1.60 |
| 7 | 220 | 100 | 3.20 |
| 15 | 475 | 250 | 8 |
| 25 | 787 | 750 | 23.80 |
| 30 | 945 | 1,500 | 47.60 |
| 50 | 1,575 | 4,000 | 127 |
| 100 | 3,150 | 10,000 | 318 |

For current exchange rates see www.xe.com

## INFORMATION

**MAURITIUS INFORMATION OFFICE**
*Mauritius Tourism Promotion Authority, 32 Elvaston Place, London SW7 5NW, Tel. +44 207 584 36 66, www.mauritius.net*

**MAURITIUS TOURISM PROMOTION AUTHORITY (MTPA)**
*11th Floor | Air Mauritius Centre | President Kennedy Street | Port Louis | tel. 210 15 45 | www.mauritius.net*

## INTERNET

At *www.airmauritius.com* the airline provides information both about flight connections to the island and helicopter tours you can take while you're there. The site also provides basic information about the country and its people. The official Tourist Office site is *www.tourism-mauritius.mu*. The ideal site for tourists is *www.mauritius.net*, providing information ranging from points of interest, a calendar of events and booking opportunities. The site *www.info-mauritius.com/english* is somewhat more business-related. When choosing accommodation, *www.mauritius.com* is helpful. The Chamber of Commerce reports in detail at www.mcci.org about every conceivable aspect of life on the island, with a focus on the economy and society. Current news can be found in the (French-language) newspapers at *www.lexpress.mu, www.lemauricien.com* and *www.lematinal.com*. You can find out about the weather on Mauritius at *http://metservice.intnet.mu* and wind and wave conditions for surfers can be found at *www.windguru.cz*.

## INTERNET CAFÉS

Most hotels offer their guests an internet connection for an additional fee. Many hotels also offer WiFi. There are internet cafés in (among others) Port Louis *(Telecom Tower | Edith Clavell Street | tel. 2 03 72 77)*, Curepipe *(Impasse Pot de Terre | tel. 6 76 18 63)*, Quatre Bornes *(Orchard Centre | tel. 4 24 05 75)* and Grand Baie *(Centre Commercial Super U)*.

## LANGUAGE

Although Creole is the language that all Mauritians master and use to speak amongst themselves, the official state language is English. This means that visitors can get by in English when out and about and in hotels. French is also widely spoken.

## MEDIA

There are three television stations that alternately broadcast in French, English and Hindi. Large hotels have their own video channels or satellite TV. English language newspapers are only available late and in the larger hotels.

## MONEY & BANKS

Rupees (1 rupee = 100 cents) can be exchanged cheaply at the airport. Cash and travellers cheques are accepted. The exchange rates in hotels are often unfavourable. There are banks in all major towns *(Mon–Thu 9.15am–3.15pm, Fri 9.15am–5pm)*. Major credit cards, which are also accepted in hotels and in larger shops, can be used to withdraw cash from ATMs.

## OPENING HOURS

Shops open from Mon to Sat between 9am and 10am and close at different times depending on the region. By western standards, everywhere closes early.

In Port Louis closing time is at 5pm; in Curepipe and other cities it's 6pm on workday evenings. On Thursdays, however, shops close at noon. In Port Louis they also close at noon on Saturdays. In most supermarkets you can shop from 7.30am to 7pm. Markets officially take place from 6am to 6pm but few stalls are open before 8am.

## PHONES & MOBILE PHONES

Dialling codes: UK 02044 and USA and Canada: 0201. Dialling code for Mauritius: 00230.

A three-minute call to Europe or the USA/Canada costs around 250 rupees from a post office or a telephone booth. Telephone cards are available from Mauritius Telecom and in shops. For local calls from a payphone you'll pay 3 rupees per minute. You can normally make direct calls from hotels. Calls received when roaming on a mobile network are usually expensive.

## PHOTOGRAPHY

It's prohibited to take pictures at the airport, in ports and around barracks. Photo equipment is more expensive on the island than at home.

## POST

There are large post offices at the harbour in Port Louis and next to the market in Curepipe. Almost every village also has one. Opening times: *Mon–Fri 8am–11am and noon–4pm, Sat 9am-11am*. Sending a postcard to Europe and the US/Canada costs up to 20 rupees, depending on the size, and a letter costs up to 40 rupees (prices are generally lower to Europe than to the American continent).

## SCOOTERS

You can now rent scooters almost everywhere and use them to explore the island. They should not be used after dark, however, and you should remain calm when you're caught up in the turmoil of the traffic in the towns. You shouldn't just rely on the indicator when you're turning, but you should also stick out your hand. Even better still, get your passenger to do it for you. If you want to turn left, stick your right arm upwards and lean it slightly to the left-hand side. When turning right, the right arm should be stretched out to the right.

## TAXI

Taxis rarely have meters. You must negotiate the price before the journey and shouldn't pay more than 40 rupees per kilometre. The journey from the airport to Port Louis costs around 2000 rupees. You can also rent taxis for the whole day.

## TIME

Time differences: Mauritius is four hours ahead of Greenwich Mean Time, ten hours ahead of US Eastern Time, and six hours behind Australian Eastern Time.

## TIPPING

Service charges and 15 per cent taxes are usually included in prices; however, a tip of up to 10 per cent is normal. Porters usually get 20 rupees per piece of luggage and maids should be given 25 rupees per day. Simply round up the amount when paying taxi drivers.

## VACCINATIONS

Although no vaccinations are required for

incoming travellers from Europe, the USA or Canada, polio, diphtheria, mumps, measles, rubella, tetanus and hepatitis A vaccinations should, however, be refreshed or taken for the first time. People travelling from areas infected with yellow fever may need a vaccination certificate. Check with your embassy if you're unsure.

## WEIGHTS & MEASURES

Kilometres and miles, kilograms and imperial pounds are still used in parallel everywhere, although the decimal system was officially introduced in 1994.

## WHAT TO WEAR

It's advisable to take light beachwear and everyday clothes with you. When in town and visiting restaurants you shouldn't wear bathing suits, and it's also considered impolite for men to go around with their shirts open. From June to September a light sweater may be necessary in the evenings. Umbrellas and raincoats should be taken on every trip to the tropics. You're not expected to wear a tie, even in luxury hotels.

## WEATHER IN MAURITIUS

| | Jan | Feb | March | April | May | June | July | Aug | Sept | Oct | Nov | Dec |
|---|---|---|---|---|---|---|---|---|---|---|---|---|
| Daytime temperatures in °C/°F | 29/84 | 29/84 | 29/84 | 28/82 | 26/79 | 25/77 | 24/75 | 24/75 | 24/75 | 25/77 | 27/81 | 29/84 |
| Nighttime temperatures in °C/°F | 22/72 | 23/73 | 22/72 | 21/70 | 19/66 | 18/64 | 17/63 | 17/63 | 17/63 | 18/64 | 20/68 | 21/70 |
| Sunshine hours/day | 8 | 8 | 7 | 7 | 6 | 6 | 6 | 6 | 7 | 7 | 8 | 8 |
| Precipitation days/month | 17 | 16 | 18 | 17 | 14 | 15 | 16 | 16 | 10 | 8 | 9 | 12 |
| Water temperature in °C/°F | 27/81 | 27/81 | 27/81 | 27/81 | 25/77 | 24/75 | 23/73 | 22/72 | 23/73 | 23/73 | 24/75 | 25/77 |

# USEFUL PHRASES FRENCH

## IN BRIEF

| | |
|---|---|
| Yes/No/Maybe | oui/non/peut-être |
| Please/Thank you | s'il vous plaît/merci |
| Good morning!/afternoon!/ evening!/night! | Bonjour!/Bonjour!/ Bonsoir!/Bonne nuit! |
| Hello!/goodbye!/See you! | Salut!/Au revoir!/Salut! |
| Excuse me, please | Pardon! |
| My name is ... | Je m'appelle ... |
| I'm from ... | Je suis de ... |
| May I ...?/ Pardon? | Puis-je ...?/Comment? |
| I would like to .../ have you got ...? | Je voudrais .../ Avez-vous? |
| How much is ...? | Combien coûte ...? |
| I (don't) like this | Ça (ne) me plaît (pas). |
| good/bad/broken | bon/mauvais/cassé |
| too much/much/little | trop/beaucoup/peu |
| all/nothing | tout/rien |
| Help!/Attention! | Au secours/attention |
| police/fire brigade/ ambulance | police/pompiers/ ambulance |
| Could you please help me? | Est-ce que vous pourriez m'aider? |
| Do you speak English? | Parlez-vous anglais? |
| Do you understand? | Est-ce que vous comprenez? |
| Could you please ...? | Pourriez vous ... s'il vous plait? |
| ... repeat that | répéter |
| ... speak more slowly | parler plus lentement |
| ... write that down | l'écrire |

## DATE & TIME

| | |
|---|---|
| Monday/Tuesday | lundi/mardi |
| Wednesday/Thursday | mercredi/jeudi |
| Friday/Saturday/ Sunday | vendredi/samedi/ dimanche |
| working day/holiday | jour ouvrable/jour férié |
| today/tomorrow/ yesterday | aujourd'hui /demain/ hier |
| hour/minute | heure/minute |
| day/night/week | jour/nuit/semaine |
| month/year | mois/année |
| What time is it? | Quelle heure est-t-il? |

# Tu parles français?

**'Do you speak French?'** This guide will help you to say the basic words and phrases in French.

| | |
|---|---|
| It's three o'clock | Il est trois heures |
| It's half past three. | Il est trois heures et demi |
| a quarter to four | quatre heures moins le quart |

## TRAVEL

| | |
|---|---|
| open/closed | ouvert/fermé |
| entrance/exit | entrée/sortie |
| departure/arrival | départ/arrivée |
| toilets/restrooms / | toilettes/ |
| ladies/gentlemen | femmes/hommes |
| (no) drinking water | eau (non) potable |
| Where is ...?/Where are ...? | Où est ...?/Où sont ...? |
| left/right | à gauche/à droite |
| straight ahead/back | tout droit/en arrière |
| close/far | près/loin |
| bus/tram/underground / taxi/cab | bus/tramway/métro/taxi |
| stop/cab stand | arrêt/station de taxi |
| parking lot/parking garage | parking |
| street map/map | plan de ville/carte routière |
| train station/harbour/ | gare/port/ |
| airport | aéroport |
| schedule/ticket | horaire/billet |
| single/return | aller simple/aller-retour |
| train/track/platform | train/voie/quai |
| I would like to rent ... | Je voudrais ... louer. |
| a car/a bicycle/ | une voiture/un vélo/ |
| a boat | un bateau |
| petrol/gas station | station d'essence |
| petrol/gas / diesel | essence/diesel |
| breakdown/repair shop | panne/garage |

## FOOD & DRINK

| | |
|---|---|
| The menu, please | La carte, s'il vous plaît. |
| Could I please have ...? | Puis-je avoir ... s'il vous plaît |
| bottle/carafe/glass | bouteille/carafe/verre |
| knife/fork/spoon | couteau/fourchette/cuillère |
| salt/pepper/sugar | sel/poivre/sucre |
| vinegar/oil | vinaigre/huile |
| milk/cream/lemon | lait/crême/citron |
| cold/too salty/not cooked | froid/trop salé/pas cuit |

| | |
|---|---|
| with/without ice/sparkling | avec/sans glaçons/gaz |
| vegetarian | végétarien(ne) |
| May I have the bill, please | Je voudrais payer, s'il vous plaît |
| bill | addition |

## SHOPPING

| | |
|---|---|
| pharmacy/chemist | pharmacie/droguerie |
| baker/market | boulangerie/marché |
| shopping centre | centre commercial |
| department store | grand magasin |
| 100 grammes/1 kilo | cent grammes/un kilo |
| expensive/cheap/price | cher/bon marché/prix |
| more/less | plus/moins |
| organically grown | de l'agriculture biologique |

## ACCOMMODATION

| | |
|---|---|
| I have booked a room | J'ai réservé une chambre |
| Do you have any ... left? | Avez-vous encore ...? |
| single room/double room | chambre simple/double |
| breakfast | petit déjeuner |
| half board/ | demi-pension/ |
| full board (American plan) | pension complète |
| shower/sit-down bath | douche/bain |
| balcony/terrace | balcon /terrasse |
| key/room card | clé/carte magnétique |
| luggage/suitcase/bag | bagages/valise/sac |

## BANKS, MONEY & CREDIT CARDS

| | |
|---|---|
| bank/ATM/pin code | banque/guichet automatique/code |
| cash/credit card | comptant/carte de crédit |
| bill/coin | billet/monnaie |

## HEALTH

| | |
|---|---|
| doctor/dentist/ | médecin/dentiste/ |
| paediatrician | pédiatre |
| hospital/emergency clinic | hôpital/urgences |
| fever/pain | fièvre/douleurs |
| diarrhoea/nausea | diarrhée/nausée |
| sunburn | coup de soleil |
| inflamed/injured | enflammé/blessé |
| plaster/bandage | pansement/bandage |
| ointment/pain reliever | pommade/analgésique |

## POST, TELECOMMUNICATIONS & MEDIA

| | |
|---|---|
| stamp | timbre |
| lettre/postcard | lettre/carte postale |
| I need a landline | J'ai besoin d'une carte téléphonique |
| phone card | pour fixe. |
| I'm looking for a prepaid card for | Je cherche une recharge |
| my mobile | pour mon portable. |
| Where can I find internet access? | Où puis-je trouver un accès à internet? |
| dial/connection/engaged | composer/connection/occupé |
| socket/charger | prise électrique/chargeur |
| computer/battery/rechargeable | ordinateur/batterie/ |
| battery | accumulateur |
| at sign (@) | arobase |
| internet address (URL)/ | adresse internet/ |
| e-mail address | mail |
| internet connection/wifi | accès internet/wi-fi |
| e-mail/file/print | mail/fichier/imprimer |

## LEISURE, SPORTS & BEACH

| | |
|---|---|
| beach | plage |
| sunshade/lounger | parasol/transat |
| low tide/high tide/current | marée basse/marée haute/courant |
| cable car/chair lift | téléphérique/télésiège |
| (rescue) hut | refuge |

## NUMBERS

| | | | |
|---|---|---|---|
| 0 | zéro | 17 | dix-sept |
| 1 | un, une | 18 | dix-huit |
| 2 | deux | 19 | dix-neuf |
| 3 | trois | 20 | vingt |
| 4 | quatre | 30 | trente |
| 5 | cinq | 40 | quarante |
| 6 | six | 50 | cinquante |
| 7 | sept | 60 | soixante |
| 8 | huit | 70 | soixante-dix |
| 9 | neuf | 80 | quatre-vingt |
| 10 | dix | 90 | quatre-vingt-dix |
| 11 | onze | 100 | cent |
| 12 | douze | 200 | deux cents |
| 13 | treize | 1000 | mille |
| 14 | quatorze | | |
| 15 | quinze | ½ | un[e] demi[e] |
| 16 | seize | ¼ | un quart |

# NOTES

Hotel: Tarisa Resort - Spa
Mont Choisy
A Man Named Ove
The Secret History

## **MARCO POLO** TRAVEL GUIDES

ALGARVE
AMSTERDAM
ATHENS
AUSTRALIA
BANGKOK
BARCELONA
BERLIN
BRAZIL
BRUSSELS
BUDAPEST
BULGARIA
CALIFORNIA
CAMBODIA
CAPE TOWN
  WINE LANDS,
  GARDEN ROUTE
CHINA
COLOGNE
COPENHAGEN
CORFU
COSTA BLANCA
  VALENCIA
COSTA DEL SOL
  GRANADA
CRETE
CUBA
CYPRUS
  NORTH AND
  SOUTH
DUBAI

DUBLIN
DUBROVNIK &
  DALMATIAN COAST
EDINBURGH
EGYPT
FINLAND
FLORENCE
FLORIDA
FRENCH ATLANTIC
  COAST
FRENCH RIVIERA
  NICE, CANNES &
  MONACO
FUERTEVENTURA
GRAN CANARIA
GREECE
HONG KONG
  MACAU
ICELAND
IRELAND
ISRAEL
ISTANBUL
JORDAN
KOS
KRAKOW
LAKE GARDA

LANZAROTE
LAS VEGAS
LISBON
LONDON
LOS ANGELES
MADEIRA
  PORTO SANTO
MADRID
MALLORCA
MALTA
  GOZO
MAURITIUS
MILAN
MOROCCO
MUNICH
NAPLES &
  THE AMALFI COAST
NEW YORK
NEW ZEALAND
NORWAY
OSLO
PARIS
PORTUGAL

PRAGUE
RHODES
ROME
SAN FRANCISCO
SARDINIA
SCOTLAND
SHANGHAI
SICILY
SINGAPORE
SOUTH AFRICA
STOCKHOLM
TENERIFE
THAILAND
TURKEY
TURKEY
  SOUTH COAST
TUSCANY
UNITED ARAB
  EMIRATES
VENICE
VIENNA
VIETNAM

- PACKED WITH INSIDER TIPS
- BEST WALKS AND TOURS
- FULL-COLOUR PULL-OUT MAP
  AND STREET ATLAS

# ROAD ATLAS

The green line ▬ indicates the Trips & Tours (p. 86–91)
The blue line ▬ indicates The perfect route (p. 30–31)

All tours are also marked on the pull-out map

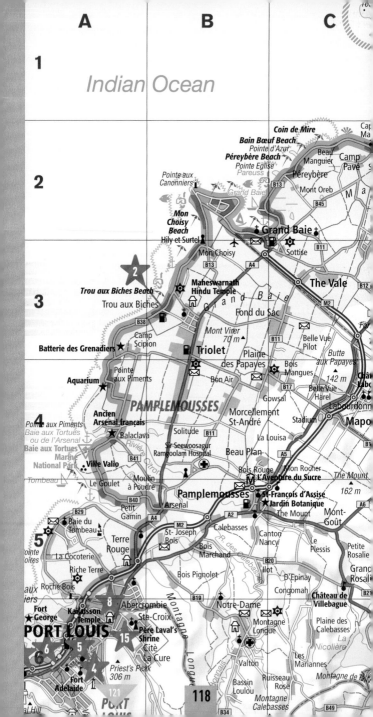

**Indian Ocean**

A B C

1

2

Coin de Mire
Bain Bœuf Beach
Pointe d'Azur
Péreybère Beach
Pointe Eglise
*Pareuss*
Pointe aux Canonniers
Grand Baie
B13

Cap
Ma

Beau
Manguier
Péreybère
Mont Oreb
Camp Pavé
B45

Ma

Mon Choisy Beach
Hily et Surtel
Mon Choisy
B13
A4

Grand Baie
Sottise
B11

3

Trou aux Biches Beach
Trou aux Biches
Maheswarnath Hindu Temple
Grand Baie
Fond du Sac

The Vale
B12

B38

Camp Scipion
Triolet
Mont Viret 70 m
Plaine des Papayes
Bon Air

M2

Belle Vue Pilot
Butte aux Papayes
142 m
Belle Vue Harel

B11

Châ
Lab

Batterie des Grenadiers
Pointe aux Piments

B11
B17

Gowsal
Morcellement St-André
Labourdonn

Mapo

Aquarium
PAMPLEMOUSSES
La Louisa
Stadium

B1

4

Ancien Arsenal français
Balaclava
Solitude B11
Sir Seewoosagur Ramgoolam Hospital
Beau Plan
A5

Pointe aux Piments
Baie aux Tortues ou de l'Arsenal
Baie aux Tortues
Marine National Park
Tombeau

Ville Valio
B41
Rivière Citron
Moulin à Poudre

Bois Rouge
Mon Rocher
L'Aventure du Sucre
St-François d'Assise
Jardin Botanique
The Mount

The Mount
162 m

A6

5

Pointe oires

Baie du Tombeau
Le Goulet
B40
Petit Gamin
B29

Pamplemousses
Arsenal
A4
M2
St-Joseph Bois
A2
Calebasses
Canton Nancy
The Mount
Mont-Goût

Le Plessis
Petite Rosalie

Terre Rouge

Bois Marchand

Grand Rosal

aux iers

La Cocoterie
Riche Terre
Roche Bois

B20

Îlot
D'Epinay
Congomah
Château de Villebague

B21

Fort George
Karlosson Temple
8
Abercrombie
Ste-Croix
Père Laval's Shrine
Cité
La Cure
Bois Pignolet
B19

Notre-Dame

Montagne Longue

Plaine des Calebasses
La Nicolière

6

PORT LOUIS
5
15
Priest's Peak 306 m
Fort Adelaide
PORT
al Hill
LOUIS

Montagne Longue

Valton

Bassin Loulou

118

Montagne Calebasses

B34

Les Mariannes

Montagne de Pou

B49

121

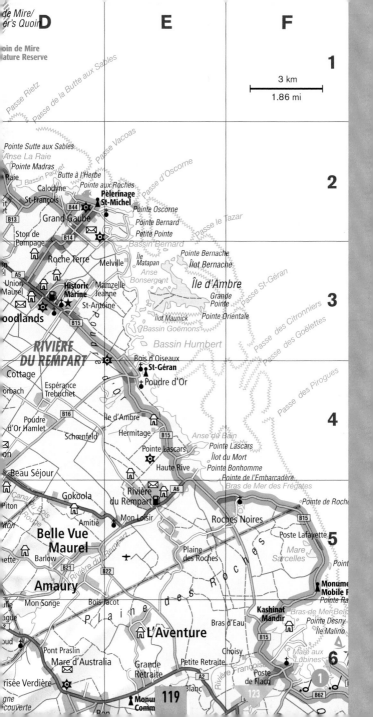

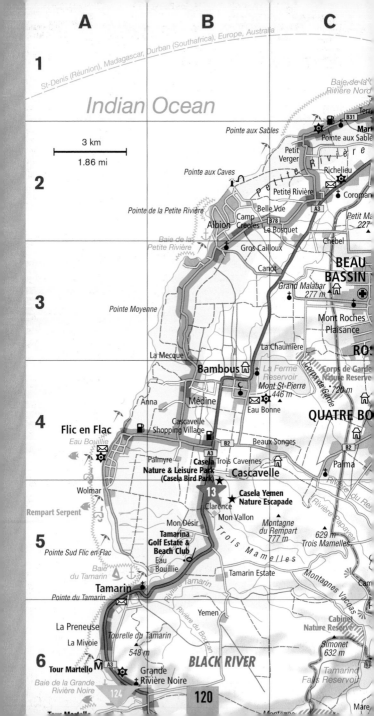

# A

## Indian Ocean

St-Denis (Réunion), Madagascar, Durban (Southafrica), Europe, Australia

3 km
1.86 mi

Pointe de la Petite Rivière

Pointe Moyenne

La Mecque

Anna

Flic en Flac
Eau Bouillie

Wolmar

Rempart Serpent

Pointe Sud Flic en Flac

Baie
du Tamarin

Tamarin
Pointe du Tamarin

La Preneuse
La Mivoie

Tourelle du Tamarin
548 m

Tour Martello

Baie de la Grande
Rivière Noire

Tour Martello

# B

Pointe aux Sables

Petit
Verger

Pointe aux Caves

Petite Rivière

Belle Vue

Camp
Créoles
Albion
Le Bosquet

Baie de la
Petite Rivière

Gros Cailloux

Canot

Bambous

La Ferme
Reservoir
Mont St-Pierre
446 m

Médine

Eau Bonne

Cascavelle
Shopping Village

Palmyre
Nature & Leisure Park
(Casela Bird Park)

Casela
Trois Cavernes

Cascavelle

13

Casela Yemen
Nature Escapade

Clarence
Mon Vallon

Mon Désir

Tamarina
Golf Estate &
Beach Club
Eau
Bouillie

Montagne
du Rempart
777 m

Trois Mamelles

Tamarin Estate

Yemen

BLACK RIVER

Grande
Rivière Noire

124

120

# C

Baie de la
Rivière Nord

B31

Mar
Pointe aux Sable

Terre

Richelieu

Coroman

A3

Petit Ma
227

Chebel

BEAU
BASSIN

Grand Malabar
277 m

Mont Roches
Plaisance

RO

Corps de Garde
Nature Reserve
720 m

QUATRE BO

Beaux Songes

B2

Palma

B2

629 m
Trois Mamelles

Montagne du Boran

Cabinet
Nature Reserve

Simonet
632 m

Tamarind
Falls Reservoir

Mare

Île aux Tonneliers
Roche Bois
Kane Terre
Bois Pignolet
D'Epinay
Longomah
Château Villebag

**D**
Fort George
Karasson Temple
Abercrombie
Ste-Croix
Montagne Longue
B19
Notre-Dame
**E**
118
Plaine de Calebas
**F**

★ **PORT LOUIS**
8
Père Laval's Shrine
Cité La Cure
Priest's Peak 306 m

15
★ ★ ★ ★
3 6 5
4
Fort Adelaide

Signal Hill 328 m
Thien-Thane
Pailles
M2

PORT LOUIS

Vallée des Prêtres
B34
Valton
Bassin Loulou
Montagne Calebasses 630 m
Crève Cœur

Les Mariannes
Ruisseau Rose
Montag
B49

Domaine Les Pailles
Pic des Guibies

Le Pouce 812 m
Pouce Nature Reserve
Pieter Both 823 m
Malenga
Ripailles
Nouvelle Découverte
2

La Laura
Roselyn Cottage
Agrément
Beau Bois
L'Avenir

**MOKA**

Eureka House Museum
7 ★
Moka
St-Pierre
Circonstance
Espérance
B51
3

Château le Réduit
Martindale
Le Réduit
Institut Mahatma Gandhi
Minissy
Helvetia
Mon Désert Alma
B48
A7
Verdun
Alma
Quart Milita

Côte d'Or
La Dagotière
B50

M2
Rivière Terre Rouge
Bagatelle

Belle Terre
Valetta Reservoir
Valetta
Vuillemin
B6

Quatre Bornes Central Market
A8
Petit Camp
Highlands
Hermitage
Verdun Hill 537 m
Montagne la Terre 504 m
4

Mauritius Glass Gallery
Camp Fouquereaux
B48
Belle Rive
Piton du Milieu 306 m
Piton du Milieu

Candos
B3
Phoenix
Galléa
B6
B62
Piton du Milieu

Square Textile Museum
Monument of the Millenium

Floreal
Trou aux Cerfs 650 m
**CUREPIPE**
La Chartreuse
5

Park
Jardin Botanique
Forest Side
M2
Domaine des Aubineaux
Montagne d'Auvillard
Midlands Dam
M i d l a n d s
Montagne Lagr
638 m

La Marie
B70
Station radio
Atélier
Seizième Mille
Coriolis
Midlands
Bananes
B86
Fressanges
6

er Nature Reserve
alls
B3
**PLAINES WILHELMS**
2
Beard
680 m
A10

Trou de Bouchet ★
570 m

121
125

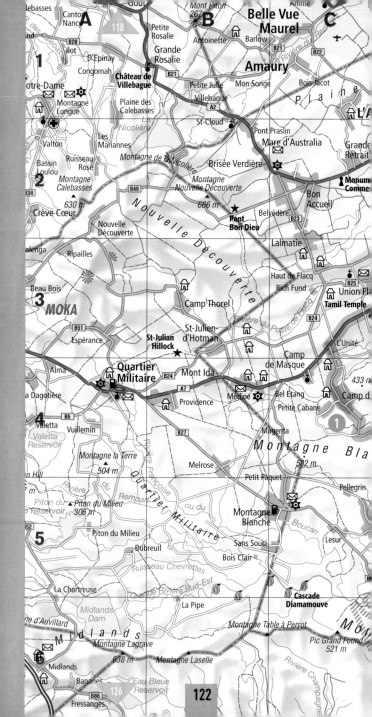

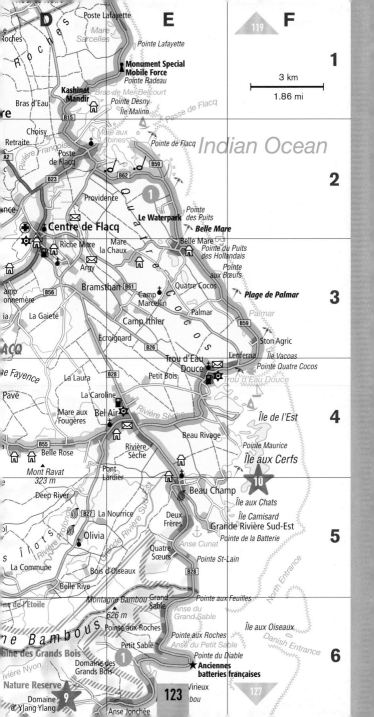

**1**

Poste Lafayette

*Mare Sarcelles*

*Pointe Lafayette*

3 km

1.86 mi

Roches

*Roches*

Bras d'Eau

*Pointe Radeau*

**Monument Special Mobile Force**

**Kashinat Mandir**

B15

*Pointe Desny*

*Bras de Mer Belcourt*

*Île Malino*

*Passe de Flacq*

**Indian Ocean**

**2**

Choisy

Retraite

*Rivière Françoise*

A2

Poste de Flacq

*Mare aux Lubines*

*Pointe de Flacq*

B23

B62

B59

Providence

**Le Waterpark**

*Pointe des Puits*

*Belle Mare*

nce

**Centre de Flacq**

Riche Mare

Mare la Chaux

Belle Mare

*Pointe du Puits des Hollandais*

Argy

*Pointe aux Bœufs*

**3**

amp

onnemère

B56

Bramsthan

B61

Quatre Cocos

*Plage de Palmar*

Camp Marcellin

Palmar

*Palmar*

ia

La Gaieté

Camp Ithier

B59

Écroignard

B26

Ston Agric

ACQ

Trou d'Eau Douce

Lenferna

*Île Vacoas*

e Fayence

La Laura

B28

Petit Bois

*Trou d'Eau Douce*

*Pointe Quatre Cocos*

Pavé

La Caroline

*Rivière Sèche*

*Île de l'Est*

**4**

Mare aux Fougères

Bel Air

Beau Rivage

*Pointe Maurice*

B55

Belle Rose

Rivière Sèche

**Île aux Cerfs**

*Mont Ravat 323 m*

Pont Lardier

**10**

Deep River

Beau Champ

*Île aux Chats*

B27

La Nourrice

Olivia

Deux Frères

*Île Camisard*

**Grande Rivière Sud-Est**

*Anse Cunat*

*Pointe de la Batterie*

**5**

Quatre Sœurs

*Pointe St-Lain*

La Commune

Bois d'Oiseaux

B28

Belle Rive

*North Entrance*

ne de l'Étoile

*Montagne Bambou 626 m*

Grand Sable

*Pointe aux Feuilles*

*Anse du Grand Sable*

*Île aux Oiseaux*

*Danish Entrance*

e Bambous

*Pointe aux Roches*

Petit Sable

*Pointe aux Roches*

*Anse du Petit Sable*

**6**

aine des Grands Bois

*Rivière Nyon*

**Nature Reserve**

Domaine des Grands Bois

*Pointe du Diable*

★ **Anciennes batteries françaises**

**9**

**123**

127

Domaine d'Ylang Ylang

Anse Jonchée

Virieux

bou

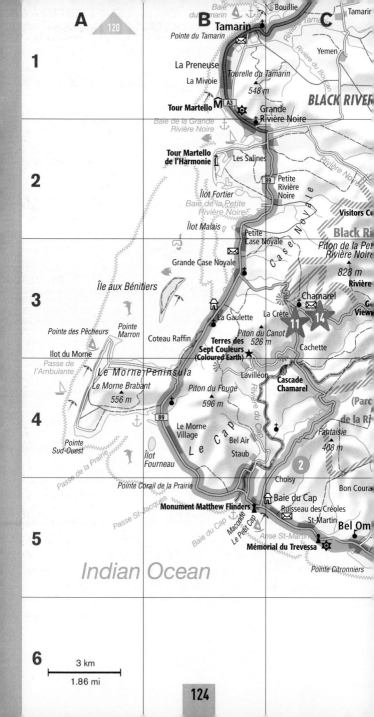

**A**  120

**B** Baie du Tamarin  Bouillie  **C** Tamar

**Tamarin**
Pointe du Tamarin

Rivière du Tamar

Yemen

**1**

La Preneuse
La Mivoie
Tourelle du Tamarin
548 m
Rivière du Boucan

**Tour Martello** M A3
Grande
† Rivière Noire

**BLACK RIVER**

Baie de la Grande
Rivière Noire

**Tour Martello
de l'Harmonie** Les Salines

**2**
B9 Petite
Rivière
Noire

Rivière Noir

Îlot Fortier
Baie de la Petite
Rivière Noire

Case Noyale

**Visitors C**

Îlot Malais
Petite
Case Noyale

**Black Ri**
Piton de la Pet
Rivière Noire

828 m

**Rivière**

Grande Case Noyale

**3**
Île aux Bénitiers

La Gaulette

**Chamarel**
La Crète

11  14

**G
View**

Pointe des Pêcheurs
Pointe
Marron
Coteau Raffin

**Terres des
Sept Couleurs
(Coloured Earth)** ★
Piton du Canot
526 m

Cachette

Îlot du Morne

Passe de
l'Ambulante

**Le Morne Peninsula**
Le Morne Brabant
556 m

Piton du Fougé
596 m

Lavilléon

**Cascade
Chamarel**

(Parc

de la Ri

**4**

Le Morne
Village
Bel Air
Staub

Fantaisie
408 m

Pointe
Sud-Ouest

B9

Îlot
Fourneau

Passe de la Prairie

Pointe Corail de la Prairie

Choisy

**2**

Bon Coura

Passe St-Jacques

**Monument Matthew Flinders**

Baie du Cap

Macondé
Le Petit Cap

**Baie du Cap**
Ruisseau des Créoles
St-Martin

Anse St-Martin

**Bel Om**

**5**

**Mémorial du Trevessa**

Pointe Citronniers

**Indian Ocean**

**6**  3 km
1.86 mi

124

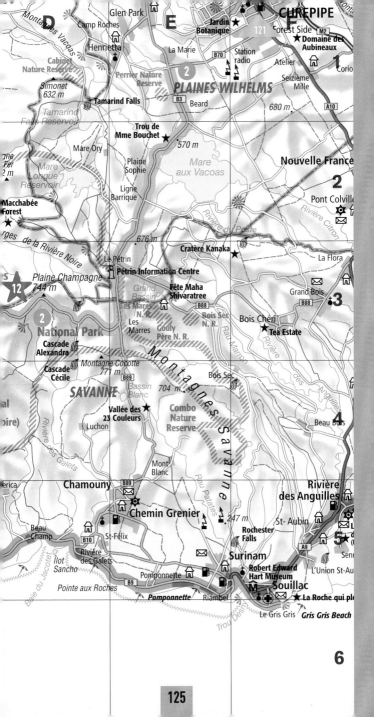

Montagnes Vacoas

**D**

Glen Park

Camp Roches

Henrietta

**E**

Jardin
Botanique ★

**F**

**CUREPIPE**

Forest Side

★ **Domaine des
Aubineaux**

121

M2

**1**

La Marie

Cabinet
Nature Reserve

B70

Atelier

Station
radio

Seizième
Mille

Corio

Simonet
632 m

Perrier Nature
Reserve

**2**

**PLAINES WILHELMS**

**Tamarind Falls**

B3

Beard

680 m

A10

Tamarind
Falls Reservoir

**Trou de
Mme Bouchet** ★

570 m

**Nouvelle France**

Mare Ory

Plaine
Sophie

Mare
aux Vacoas

**2**

ne
Fer
2 m

Mare
Longue
Reservoir

Ligne
Barrique

Pont Colvill

Rivière Citron

**Macchabée
Forest**

676 m

Rivière du Poste

☒

rges

de la Rivière Noire

Le Pétrin

**Cratère Kanaka** ★

La Flora

★
**12**

**Plaine Champagne**
744 m

**Pétrin Information Centre**

Grand
Bassin
N. R.

**Fête Maha
Shivaratree** ★

B88

Grand Bois

B88

☒

‡**3**

**2**

**National Park**

Les
Marres

Gouly
Père N. R.

**Bois Sec
N. R.**

**Bois Chéri**
★ **Tea Estate**

Rau Marron

Rivière

des

**Cascade
Alexandra**

Montagne Cocotte
771 m

B89

**Cascade
Cécile**

Bassin
Blanc

Bois Sec

704 m

Montagnes Savanne

Anguilles

**SAVANNE**

**Vallée des
23 Couleurs** ★

Luchon

**Combo
Nature
Reserve**

Beau Bois

**4**

al
pire)

Rivière des Galets

Mont
Blanc

Rau Patates

Chamouny

B89

**Rivière
des Anguilles**

erica

247 m

St- Aubin

☒

☒

**5**★

**Chemin Grenier**

**Rochester
Falls**

A9

Senr

Beau
Champ

St-Félix

B10

**Robert Edward
Hart Museum**

L'Union St-Au

Rivière
des Galets

☒

**Surinam**

Îlot
Sancho

Pomponnette

B9

**M**

**Souillac**

☒

★ **La Roche qui pl**

Pointe aux Roches

**Pomponnette**

Riambel

Le Gris Gris

**Gris Gris Beach**

Baie du Jacotet

Trou D'Est

**6**

125

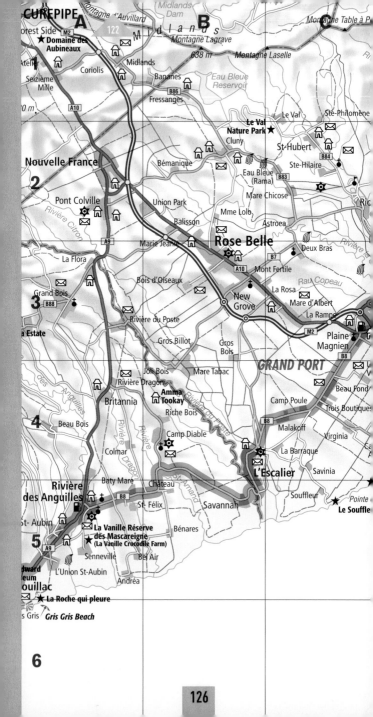

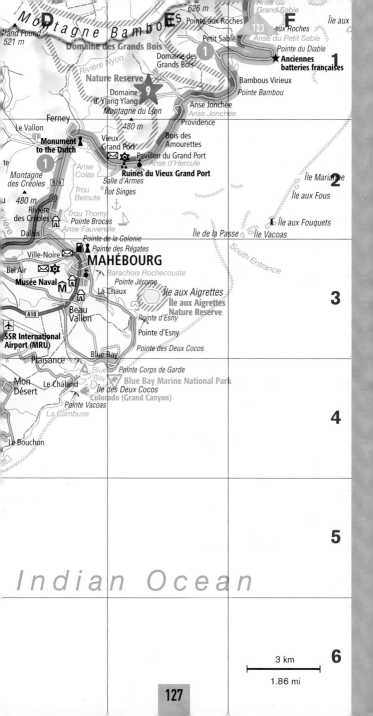

**Montagne Bamboes**

626 m
Pointe aux Roches
Anse du Grand Sable
Île aux

Grand Found
521 m

Domaine des Grands Bois

Petit Sablé
Anse du Petit Sable
Pointe du Diable

123
aux Roches

Domaine des Grands Bois

Rivière Nyon

**Nature Reserve** 9

Domaine d'Ylang Ylang
Montagne du Lion
480 m

Anse Jonchée
Anse Jonchée

★ **Anciennes batteries françaises**

Bambous Virieux
Pointe Bambou

**F**

**1**

Ferney

Le Vallon

**Monument to the Dutch** 1

te

Montagne des Créoles
B28
480 m

Rivière des Créoles

Dalais

Vieux Grand Port
Anse Colas
Salle d'Armes
Trou Beloute
Îlot Singes

Providence
Bois des Amourettes

Pavillon du Grand Port
Anse d'Hercule
**Ruines du Vieux Grand Port**

Île Mariane
Île aux Fous

**2**

Trou Thomy
Pointe Brocus
Anse Fauverelle
Pointe de la Colonie
Pointe des Régates

Île de la Passe
Île aux Fouquets
Île Vacoas

Ville-Noire

Bel Air
**Musée Naval** M

**MAHÉBOURG**

Barachois Rochecouste
Pointe Jérôme

South Entrance

**3**

La Chaux

Beau Vallon
A10

**SSR International Airport (MRU)**

Plaisance

Pointe d'Esny

Île aux Aigrettes
**Île aux Aigrettes Nature Reserve**
Pointe d'Esny
Pointe des Deux Cocos

Blue Bay

Mon Désert
Le Chaland

Pointe Vacoas
La Cambuse

Pointe Corps de Garde
Blue Bay
**Blue Bay Marine National Park**
Île des Deux Cocos
**Colorado (Grand Canyon)**

**4**

Le Bouchon

**5**

*Indian Ocean*

3 km

1.86 mi

**6**

# KEY TO ROAD ATLAS

| | |
|---|---|
| ══ M2 ╪═ Autobahn mit Anschlussstelle<br>Motorway with junction | ⚓ ⛵ Hafen; Segeln<br>Port; sailing |
| ═ ═ ═ Autobahn in Bau<br>Motorway under construction | 🐟 Hochseefischen; Fischen<br>Deep sea fishing; fishing |
| ▬▬▬ Fernstraße<br>Highway | 🔺🤿 Wassersport; gute Schnorchelmöglichkeit<br>Watersports; snorkel possibility |
| ▬▬▬ Hauptstraße<br>Main road | ☀ ◀ Aussichtspunkt<br>Lookout point |
| ⋯⋯⋯ Nebenstraße<br>Secondary road | ⚑ 🗼 Leuchtturm; Turm<br>Lighthouse; tower |
| ▬ ▬ ▬ Fahrweg; Fußweg<br>Track; footpath | 📡 Sendeturm<br>Telecommunication tower |
| wwwww Korallenriff<br>Coral reef | ♟ ♟ Schloss, Burg; Kirche<br>Palace, castle; church |
| ▬ ▬ ▬ Fähre<br>Ferry | ⚑ 🏛 Moschee; Tempel<br>Mosque; temple |
| ▬▬▬ Provinzgrenze<br>Province border | ⌓ ★ Höhle; Sehenswürdigkeit<br>Cave; point of interest |
| ///////// Nationalpark<br>National park | ▲ · Berggipfel; Höhenpunkt<br>Mountain top; geodetic point |
| ✈ Internationaler Flughafen<br>International airport | ∴ Ⓜ Archäologische Stätte; Museum<br>Archeological site; museum |
| ✈ Flugplatz<br>Airfield | ▮ Denkmal, Monument<br>Memorial, mounument |
| 🏖 Badestrand<br>Beach | 🌊 Wasserfall<br>Waterfall |
| ▬▬▬ Ausflüge und Touren<br>Trips & Tours | ✚ ✡ Krankenhaus; Polizei<br>Hospital; police |
| ▬▬▬ Perfekte Route<br>Perfect route | ✉ ⛽ Postamt; Tankstelle<br>Post office; filling station |

MARCO POLO Highlights

# INDEX

This index lists all of the places and attractions, plus some of the points of interest, people, and terms featured in this guide. Numbers in bold indicate a main entry.

# CREDITS

# WRITE TO US

e-mail: info@marcopologuides.co.uk

Did you have a great holiday?
Is there something on your mind?
Whatever it is, let us know!
Whether you want to praise, alert us to errors or give us a personal tip –
MARCO POLO would be pleased to hear from you.
We do everything we can to provide the very latest information for your trip.

Nevertheless, despite all of our authors' thorough research, errors can creep in. MARCO POLO does not accept any liability for this. Please contact us by e-mail or post.

MARCO POLO Travel Publishing Ltd
Pinewood, Chineham Business Park
Crockford Lane, Chineham
Basingstoke, Hampshire RG24 8AL
United Kingdom

**PICTURE CREDITS**
Cover Photograph: Look: (Morne Brabant, Paradise Beach) age fotostock
Images: Domaine Anna (17 bottom); Huber: Achmann (36), Huber (104 bottom), Mezzanotte (3 top, 58/59), Puku (96/97), Scatè (75), Schmid (3 centre, 4, 10/11, 23, 28, 29, 44/45, 63, 68/69), Giovanni Simeone (60, 83); R. Irek (2 centre top, 6, 54, 100/101); iStockphoto.com: Raido Väljamaa (16 centre); Kitezone Ltd: Marianne Erne Nobin (16 bottom); Laif: Biskup (right flap); 18/19, 28/29, 52), Buss/Hoa-Qui (9), Guichaoua/Hoa/Qui (30 r.), hemis.fr (42), hemis.fr (Degas) (left flap, 3 bottom, 27, 76/77), hemis.fr (Rieger) (7), Heuer (12, 26 l., 26 r., 92/93), Huber (101, 104 top), Jonkmanns (57, 64), Le Figaro Magazine (Prignet) (39), Meier (40, 91, 94, 100), Standl (48), Tophoven (2 centre bottom, 24/25, 32/33); F. Langer (1 bottom); Look: age fotostock (1 top, 2 bottom, 46/47, 86/87), Kreuzer (30 l.), Maeritz (2. top, 5); mauritius images: Alamy (80, 84/85), Cassio (78), imagebroker (Gerhard) (70); H. Mielke (8, 13, 15, 20, 34, 41, 50/51, 67, 72/73, 88, 90, 99, 105, 120/121); Tamarin Ocean Pro Diving (17 top); Veranda Resorts (16 top)

**1st Edition 2013**
Worldwide Distribution: Marco Polo Travel Publishing Ltd, Pinewood, Chineham Business Park, Crockford Lane, Basingstoke, Hampshire RG24 8AL, United Kingdom. Email: sales@marcopolouk.com
© MAIRDUMONT GmbH & Co. KG, Ostfildern
Chief editors: Michaela Lienemann (concept, managing editor), Marion Zorn (concept, text editor)
Author: Freddy Langer; Editor: Franziska Kahl
Programme supervision: Anita Dahlinger, Ann-Katrin Kutzner, Nikolai Michaelis
Picture editors: Gabriele Forst, Barbara Schmid; What's hot: wunder media, Munich;
Cartography road atlas: DuMont Reisekartografie, Fürstenfeldbruck; © MAIRDUMONT, Ostfildern
Cartography pull-out map: DuMont Reisekartografie, Fürstenfeldbruck; © MAIRDUMONT, Ostfildern
Design: milchhof : atelier, Berlin; Front cover, pull-out map cover, page 1: factor product munich
Translated from German by Jonathan Andrews, Mainz; editor of the English edition: Neil Williamson, Wilmslow
Prepress: BW-Medien GmbH, Leonberg
Phrase book in cooperation with Ernst Klett Sprachen GmbH, Stuttgart, Editorial by Pons Wörterbücher

# DOS & DON'TS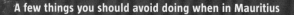

**A few things you should avoid doing when in Mauritius**

## COLLECTING DODGY SOUVENIRS

Shells, coral and turtles belong in the sea and not gathering dust on a shelf! If you collect or buy any of these items, you're partly responsible for the destruction of a unique, fragile underwater world. Whether they're dead or alive, from other countries or from the island, bred in captivity or not – leave them well alone. Many a souvenir is confiscated by customs authorities at the border because of the ban on imports.

## EXPECTING WESTERN CONDITIONS

Despite the highways and traffic lights, Mauritius isn't a western country. This means, particularly at night, that you should not just focus on the traffic (which drives on the left). The island's streets are full of obstacles at all hours, including potholes, unlit bicycles, drunken labourers and sleeping dogs. Incidentally, you should always sign in when you visit a large hotel, otherwise you risk being barred by the porter.

## GOING TOPLESS

On public beaches, where local women even keep their saris on in the water, the population finds tight swimwear or topless sunbathers offensive. Nude bathing is forbidden, though topless bathing is usually tolerated in the pool complexes of the larger hotels. Only take bikini tops off when you're sure there are only other tourists around.

## DRIVING PRICES DOWN

The price differences between staying in a hotel and living in a village are enormous. For an overnight stay with half-board in a double room, holiday-makers often pay more than a Mauritian person earns in a month. For some self-appointed guides, this is reason enough to set their rates to a 'western' standard. You should, therefore, always pre-arrange prices and ask about the going rates in hotels (such as, for example, the price of taxis) – this will save you some nasty surprises. When taking tours of temple complexes, a donation is expected, and you won't make any friends if you don't give at least 20 rupees.

## BEING CARELESS

If you've rented private accommodation, it's advisable to close your doors and windows when going to bed or when leaving the house. Don't leave your valuables and money lying around.

## REVEALING TOO MUCH BARE FLESH

Even on the street and in restaurants it's considered impolite to go around in overly revealing casual wear. In temples, and to an even greater extent in mosques, visitors are expected to wear long trousers and long sleeved shirts. Shoes must be taken off at the entrance.